Glimpses of

Prayer

Shirley Crowder

&

Harriet E. Michael

Illustrated by Kristin Michael

Published by:

Pix-N-Pens Publishing
PO Box 702852
Dallas, TX 75370
www.WriteIntegrity.com

Printed in the United States of America

Dedication

We dedicate this book
to Mrs. Athalea Godwin,
a dear friend
and sweet encourager
to us and so many others.

Table of Contents

Preface

I looked for someone among them who would build up the wall and stand before me in the gap on behalf of the land so I would not have to destroy it, but I found no one.

Ezekiel 22:30 (NIV)

One of the primary means Christ-followers use to communicate with God is through prayer. The other is the Word of God—the Bible. God is looking for prayer warriors—men and women who will call on Him and stand in the gap before Him, lifting up situations, circumstances, praises, catastrophes, and concerns in their prayers.

We, the authors, are grateful to be collaborating on another devotional. This ten-week collection is centered around prayer. Each devotion focuses on verses in the Bible that speak about prayer. Harriet E. Michael wrote the devotions from the Old Testament, and Shirley Crowder wrote the devotions from the New Testament. The devotional weeks alternate between the New Testament and the Old Testament.

We hope these devotions will lead you to not only have a better understanding of prayer, but that the Holy Spirit would use the devotions to ignite or deepen your passion to know Him better, and that your prayer life would become richer.

We are thankful for Kristin Michael's (Harriet's daughter) beautiful illustrations for this devotional.

We appreciate the wise input and editorial advice our fellow Nigeria Missionary Kid, Baker Hill, provided.

We are also grateful to our publisher, Marji Laine Clubine, for the beautiful cover design and her encouragement and direction, which were invaluable throughout the whole process of writing and publishing this devotional

.

Chapter One:

Jesus Models Prayer

Shirley

A Mighty Prayer Warrior
Ephesians 6:10-20

First of all, then, I urge that supplications, prayers, intercessions, and thanksgivings be made for all people.
1 Timothy 2:1

My mom was a pray-er. She had an ongoing conversation with God throughout the day. I would often ask her to repeat something I had only partially heard her say, and she would respond, "I was talking to God, not you." She would be listening to the news and hear a story that mentioned a specific place that brought to mind a friend, and she would say aloud, "Lord, watch over (person's name). I'm not sure what's going on, but You are."

Sometimes we'd run into someone she knew who would share a struggle that concerned them, and Mom would stop right there—in the pharmacy aisle or restroom or parking lot or wherever she was—and pray aloud for that person. Often during the last several years of Mom's life as I walked down the hallway at night, I'd stop at the corner near her room and listen as she prayed aloud. She prayed by name for all of her children, grandchildren, sisters, other extended family, the Nigeria Mission family, and countless friends. She didn't just pray, "God, take care of…" She prayed specifically concerning the things of which she was aware that each person was going through.

One morning many years ago when I lived in a different state from Mom, I called to ask her to pray about a meeting that I would soon be in. I gave the high points of a difficult situation with two people whom I supervised. Mom said, "Well, I will pray for you the way I always do when I know you've got an important meeting or are speaking somewhere. I pray that the Lord would clamp your mouth shut like He did the lions in the den when you shouldn't speak, and give you boldness to speak the truth in love when you need to."

Someone like my mom, who diligently and fervently prays, is called a prayer warrior. What image comes to your mind when you think of a warrior? I think of the armor-clad men of medieval times, or of someone who courageously stands prepared, protected, armed, and ready for battle.

A prayer warrior is a Christ-follower who is aware of the spiritual battle occurring around him or her at all times, and who frequently and consistently prays to the Father.

Since the life of Jesus Christ serves as an example of how Christ-followers are to live, we should imitate His prayer life. Jesus was, and is, the ultimate model of a prayer warrior as He showed us how to pray. We sometimes find it hard to grasp that prayer was an integral part of the life of Jesus while He lived on earth as fully God and fully man. During that time, He taught all those who followed Him how to pray.

Jesus prayed before making important decisions such as whom He would choose as His disciples (Luke 6:12). He prayed thanking God for His provision, like the time He prayed before dividing the two loaves and three fishes that fed the multitude (John 6:11). Jesus prayed when facing horrendous circumstances such as when He asked His Heavenly Father to make it possible for Him not to face the impending torture, crucifixion, and death.

And, He prayed that His Father's will would be done in and through every situation (Mark 14:36).

We all know men and women whom we call our prayer warriors; those whom we know are faithful and powerful prayers. How did they become powerful prayer warriors?

A prayer warrior is a Christ-follower who knows God through faithfully reading, studying, memorizing, meditating upon, and contemplating His Word. He or she has also been faithful to obey and live out that Word. As a result of knowing God and His character so well, a prayer warrior lifts concerns up to God, trusting that He is able to answer prayers when they are in line with His will. And, a prayer warrior is someone on whom you can always depend to pray for the things you mention to them, the things they become aware of, or the things that the Lord lays upon their hearts. They pray throughout the day about everything that they think, hear, see, or experience.

Prayer: Father, as I read, study, memorize, meditate upon, and contemplate Your Word, help me know You so that I will trust You, strengthen me to be obedient to Your Word and to trust You, as in prayer I bring my petitions to You, in the name of Jesus. Amen.

Ponder this: The depth of our prayer life is directly linked to the level of our commitment to knowing God through His Word and in prayer. God gifted and enabled some Christ-followers to be mighty prayer warriors, and, it is the job of each Christ-follower to develop into a prayer warrior. What do you need to do to become a mighty prayer warrior?

Day 2
Lord, Teach Us to Pray
Matthew 6:5-13

One day, Jesus was praying in a certain place.
When he finished, one of his disciples said to him,
"Lord, teach us to pray, just as John taught his disciples."
Luke 11:1 (NIV)

As a child, it struck me as odd that the disciples had to ask Jesus to teach them to pray. After all, they were the disciples, the ones whom Jesus chose to follow Him, those He taught throughout His time here on earth, His closest friends and confidants.

Then, when I was a teenager, a young man whom I'll call John began attending the church my Dad pastored. After about nine months, he came to Christ and joined the church. Not long after that time, this young man was part of a group of young people who were at our house for supper. When it came time to thank the Lord for our meal, my dad asked if anyone wanted to pray.

The young man spoke up and said, "I want to pray, but I can't pray all those fancy prayers most people pray. I don't know what to say."

It was a great opportunity for my parents to teach all of us about prayer. Through Bible study and the example of godly men and women, this young man began to learn that prayer is a conversation with God, and that the attitude of a person's heart is more important than the words he speaks.

Our verses for today are often referred to as "The Lord's Prayer." While the Lord prayed this prayer, it was actually a sample or model prayer He prayed to demonstrate to and teach the disciples how to pray. So, it may be more accurate to call it "The Pattern of Prayer."

While Harriet and I were growing up on the mission field in Nigeria, my mom and Harriet's mom made all our clothes. They were wonderful seamstresses. They would stock up on patterns when we were home in the States for furlough, and relatives would send the newest fashion patterns to us from time to time. Not only did I, my sister, Harriet, and her sisters wear beautiful homemade clothes, our dolls had the most beautiful clothes, lined jackets and slacks, fashioned after the "real people" patterns. I can still remember a beautiful pink satin evening gown one of my dolls wore.

According to the site for Merriam Webster, a pattern is "something designed or used as a model for making things."

When we tune in to the radio, television, or Internet, we hear and read many things about prayer that are completely unbiblical, as people take certain verses from the Bible out of context. People have so many ideas about prayer—you have to close your eyes, you have to bow your head, or you have to kneel—to name just a few. Each of these has valid applications, so we study the pattern for prayer that Jesus gave us to know how to pray and for what we should pray.

Jesus begins His teaching by reminding us that we are to have a humble attitude when we pray, that we are not to do things in our praying that bring attention to ourselves, and that we are not to pray by repeating meaningless words. Our praying indicates our recognition of God the Father and God the Savior Son. The more we come to know Him through reading, memorizing, studying, contemplating, and meditating upon His Word, the more we will trust Him as we pray.

Then, because we know Him and trust Him, we are able to lay our requests before Him and pray that He will answer those prayers according to His will. When Jesus tells us to pray, "your kingdom come, your will be done, on earth as it is in Heaven," He is telling us that our prayers are channels through which God's preordained plans come to fruition. He also tells us that the purpose of our prayers is for God's work to be done in Heaven and on earth, not for our own selfish gratification.

As Jesus continues, He tells us to pray in recognition of our absolute dependence upon God. We pray for our daily needs to be met, for forgiveness of our sins, and for spiritual protection.

When we come to God in prayer, we are intentionally asking God into every part of our being, and we pray according to His will because we know He knows everything about us, and He knows every need and desire we have.

Prayer: Our Heavenly Father, thank You for Your Holy Spirit-inspired Word through which we come to know and trust You. Give us a passion to communicate more with You through prayer. In the name of Jesus, we pray. Amen.

Ponder this: The Creator, the All-Powerful Sovereign God of the universe, invites us to communicate with Him and bring all our cares and concerns to Him in prayer. What things are keeping you from trusting God enough to bring all your cares and concerns to Him in prayer?

Come Unto Me
Matthew 11:25-30

"Come to me, all you who labor and are heavy laden,
and I will give you rest."
Matthew 11:28 (NKJV)

At the pharmacy one day, a little tow-headed, blue-eyed boy caught my eye. He was accompanying his mom and his baby sister as he trudged alongside the stroller. I noticed him because he was trying to carry an enormous pink diaper bag.

I moved close enough to hear his mom say, "Sweetheart, let Mommy carry that."

"No," he said, "I can do it!"

He was struggling with all his might to carry this heavy burden. He put the bag on the floor and gathered the long handles, pulled them up on his shoulder (as he had likely seen his parents do) and tried to walk forward, but was snapped backward because the bag was dragging across the floor.

Again, his mom said, "Are you sure you don't want me to carry that?"

His stern "No!" was met with a cautionary glance from his mom, so he said, "No, ma'am. No!"

About that time his dad walked up and said, "Son, I'll carry that," to which the child replied, "Dad, I'm trying!"

Next, he decided if he put his arms through the straps he could carry it like a backpack, but alas, the long straps allowed the bag to just drag along the floor.

In utter defeat, the little boy sat down on the floor and began crying, "It's too heavy!"

With seemingly little effort, the dad scooped up his son and the bag, putting one of the long straps over his shoulder and another over the shoulder of his son.

He said, "You see buddy, when you don't try to do things all by yourself, they are easier and you can carry very heavy things!"

I tried not to be too conspicuous as I followed this little family through the various aisles listening as this dad explained to his son how God can and will help us carry things that are heavy (burdens). The dad continued by telling the little boy that whenever something makes him angry or sad, he can talk to God about it.

What a blessing to witness this wonderful example of how we Christ-followers often struggle to carry our burdens instead of talking to God about them and receiving His wisdom, discernment, encouragement, grace, mercy, strength, and help to carry them.

What an incredible example of an earthly father teaching his son about the Heavenly Father! And the earthly son listening and receiving rest from his burden as he learned that Father God can and will carry any burden we have.

In the chapters preceding Matthew 11, we read of the growing hostility toward Jesus and His declaration that He was the Son of God. The first few verses in Matthew 11 tell of John the Baptist sending his disciples to ask Jesus, "Are you the coming one, or do we look for another?" (NKJV). Jesus tells the messengers to go back to John and tell him everything they were hearing and seeing. In Matthew 11:20-24, Jesus "began to rebuke the cities in which most of His mighty works had been done, because they did not repent" (NKJV) and tell them of the judgment that was coming to them because they did not believe He was the Son of God.

In today's passage, Jesus is responding to those who are so hostile toward Him. He begins praying to His Heavenly Father, then invites those who have been hostile—the unbelievers—to come to Him and become a part of the Kingdom of God.

Jesus' invitation was for everyone, and those coming to a saving knowledge of Him do so only by God's truth being revealed to them.

In context, our focal passage is a call for unbelievers "who labor and are heavy laden" with their sin to come to Him for spiritual rest. Then, Jesus contrasts His yoke, which is light, with the heavy yoke of the Pharisees' hypocritical regulations.

Jesus' invitation also has an application for Christ-followers who have become burdened by the weight of unconfessed sin. Jesus says, "Come" and "I will give you rest."

Prayer: Father God, thank You that as unbelievers, we are able to come to You for salvation. And, once we come to a saving knowledge of You, we can continually come and lay our burdens upon You and receive rest for our weary souls. In the name of Jesus, I pray. Amen.

Ponder this: How often do you and I struggle to carry a heavy load just like the little boy in this account? We often try to figure things out on our own, yet we usually fail miserably, until we come to Christ with our burdens and concerns. What burdens are you carrying that you need to lay upon Jesus?

Jesus the Intercessor—Then and Now

Read: John 17:20-26

*Therefore he is able to save completely those
who come to God through him,
because he always lives to intercede for them.*
Hebrews 7:25 (NIV)

Many decades ago, I came home from elementary school, very upset by something I had heard on the playground that day. One of my friends told another friend that she was praying for his dad who was in the hospital.

The boy said, "We don't need you to pray for us, Jesus is praying for us!"

My friend argued with him that she did need to pray for them because her momma told her to! And, she went on to explain that Jesus was too busy to pray for them!

Well, I wasn't exactly sure what was going on, but I knew enough to know that something was very wrong with what I was overhearing! So, I came home and told my dad that we needed to talk.

As I unloaded all the pertinent facts, including my "wise" conclusions about each fact, my dad listened intently. I told him I thought they were both wrong and that he needed to tell them about Jesus so they would go to heaven. And, I added with a great deal of confidence, "I know Jesus is busy, but He is never too busy for me or anyone else!"

Dad carefully and lovingly addressed each of my concerns and took me to the John 17 passage you read today as he explained that Jesus prayed for the disciples who were there with Him at the Last Supper as they shared a meal together.

It was in the upper room setting that Jesus prayed what some call "The Disciples' Prayer" or "The High Priestly Prayer" that we find in John 17. In this prayer, Jesus looked toward Heaven and prayed aloud for God's glory to be manifested in and through Him. Jesus prayed for His disciples to continue serving Him, for their protection from attacks of the evil one, and that they would be sanctified (made into the image of Christ) by God's truth.

Dad also talked about the passages that tell us Christ is sitting at the right hand of the throne of God interceding for us. And, he explained that Jesus invited us to pray.

Then, Dad explained the passage we read today, where we see that when He walked on earth Jesus prayed for me, you, and all Christ-followers.

Jesus prayed for the people who would come to Christ as a result of the ministry of the disciples, and for those in the future—including us, right now—who would come to faith in Jesus Christ. He prayed for spiritual unity among Christ-followers so that we would well represent Jesus Christ to the world. He prayed that Christ-followers would be made perfect in oneness, or have perfect spiritual unity. Jesus also asked God to enable the world to believe that the Father sent Him.

Jesus ended by praying that the love God had for Him would be in all of us—that He and His love would dwell within Christ-followers for God's glory.

Today's focal passage makes it clear that the basis of Christ's intercession is His finished work on the cross that satisfied God's demand. Christ continually intercedes for us—even now. Imagine that! Christ's sacrifice on the cross was a one-time sacrifice that did not need to be offered over and over as did the annual sacrifices we read about in the Old Testament and parts of the New Testament.

What an encouragement for to know that Jesus Christ the Son of God is interceding for us. This is another biblical truth that can help struggling Christ-followers come to God in prayer. For those who are burdened because of life-dominating sin or false guilt, Jesus interceding for us helps assure us we are forgiven and loved by God. Through His intercession, our confidence and assurance that God is at work in and through our situation will grow.

God has invited us to pray to Him. He is able to answer our prayers and does so according to His will.

Prayer: Father, we thank You for praying for us, and for showing us how to pray. Thank You that in our weakness when we don't know how or what to pray, You intercede for us with "groanings that cannot be uttered" (Romans 8:26 NKJV).

Ponder this: What difference would it make in your life if you recognized that Jesus Christ prayed, and is praying, for you? In what situations would your awareness of Jesus' intercession alleviate anxiety or fear?

Jesus Prayed When Grieving
Read: John 11:28-37

When Jesus heard it (about the death of John the Baptist), *He departed from there by boat to a deserted place by Himself.*
Matthew 14:13a (NIV)

Part of my childhood was spent in Nigeria, West Africa, where my parents were missionaries. Many things about the people and culture are still very clear in my mind, even after several decades!

I remember one of the customs in Nigeria (and many other parts of the world). When a loved one dies, mourners—often paid professional mourners—would be at the home of the deceased. They wail and cry loudly and continually. Having many loud mourners is a sign that the deceased was well-loved.

Thinking of these professional mourners make me think of 1 Thessalonians 4:13, and how grateful I am that when Christ-followers grieve, we do not grieve like those with no hope.

Our American culture has a myriad of ways to express grief when a loved one dies, a job is lost, a relationship ends, and other losses are experienced. Sadly, some of our expressions of grief over our losses closely resemble the pagan professional mourners' practices.

What can we understand about prayer from the way Jesus responded to grief? From Scripture, we know He responded in absolute faith in God, His Heavenly Father. As Christ-followers, we too can exercise faith in God and rely upon the Holy Spirit for the strength and comfort we need to walk through our grief.

Let's look at some of the times in the New Testament that Jesus grieved and see what we can learn about praying when we are grieved.

Luke 22:42-44 gives us a couple of insights into how Jesus grieved. One of the first things we notice when Jesus was grieved is that He trusted God. Because of His relationship with His Heavenly Father, Jesus knew God's character and faithfulness and was able to trust the Father. Another thing we see in this passage is the close, honest relationship Jesus had with His Father.

Through Christ's example, we are reminded to work on our relationship with God by reading, studying, memorizing, meditating upon, and contemplating His Word as we consistently and honestly communicate with Him through prayer.

Matthew 14:13-17 tells us what Jesus did when His cousin, John the Baptist, was killed. First of all, He went off to be by Himself with His Father for comfort and strength. This doesn't mean that anytime we want to pray we have to go off alone; however, when our world is badly shaken, it is good to pull away and have a time of prayer for comfort, strength, and wisdom from our Heavenly Father.

Another interesting thing we notice in this passage is that after spending some time alone with God in prayer, Jesus returned to the crowds and ministered to them. When we are grieving, many of us do not even think about ministering to other people, do we? Yet, that is precisely what Jesus did. Through His time alone with God, Jesus received the comfort He needed from His Father and gained strength to continue doing what He was called to do—minister to hurting people. When we are grieving, it is only by the grace of God, who supplies our every need, that we are able to minister to others through the power of God.

In today's passage, we read how Jesus responded when He learned that his friend Lazarus had died… "Jesus wept" (John 11:35). Jesus' reaction to this news used to be perplexing to me. After all, Jesus traveled there specifically to raise Lazarus from the dead. It wasn't a surprise to Him that Lazarus died, so why did He weep?

I remember asking my daddy that very question. Here are the things that stuck in my mind from Dad's explanation. Jesus had compassion for anyone who was suffering; Jesus wept over the disaster sin wreaks in our lives; Jesus wept over the unbelief of the people around Him, Jesus wept because of the weight of what was to happen just a few days later—His own death on the cross.

Once again, Jesus turned to His Heavenly Father in prayer and then raised Lazarus from the dead.

Prayer: Heavenly Father, thank You for Your Son's example of coming to You when we grieve. We are grateful that You are always ready and able to comfort and strengthen us. Help us know You better so that we will trust You more, in Jesus' name. Amen.

Ponder this: Over what are you grieving today? Christ showed us how to have hope when we grieve. In the midst of our sorrow, God's grace, comfort, and strength enable us to minister to others, and in doing so, we too are strengthened.

Chapter Two
The Psalms

Harriet

The Greatest Privilege

Read: Psalm 4

*Call to me and I will answer you and tell you great and
unsearchable things you do not know.*

Jeremiah 33:3 (NIV)

Many years ago, my family took a trip to visit my oldest son
who lived in the Washington, DC, area at the time. On our way
home, we stopped at the Manassas National Battlefield site in
Manassas, Virginia, just outside of Washington, DC. It's a Civil
War battlefield. While visiting the gift shop, I picked up a book
entitled, *Soldiers of the Cross* written by Kent D. Dollar and
began thumbing through it.

I happened to read a page where Dollar told of a hand-
written journal that had belonged to a Civil War soldier named
Edward Owings Guerrant. In the journal, the soldier had written
these words, "Prayer moves the arm that moves the universe…
Prayer is the greatest privilege man can have."

The words struck me. Standing in that gift shop, a mental
picture formed in my mind of a soldier in the throes of war,
sitting by himself contemplating prayer and writing about it in his
journal. In my mind, I saw him sitting underneath the shade of a
tree with his journal resting on his lap. It was summertime when
we visited this historic site, so I pictured the man writing in his
journal in the heat of the summer, green leaves above his head.
Many questions filled my mind. Did he survive the war? Did he

get to go back home to his family? Was he able to rebuild his life after that tragic chapter in our nation's history?

I will never know the answers to these questions in my lifetime, but this I know—in the privacy of his personal quiet time, he penned a beautiful statement about prayer. One that impacted others, like me, long after his death. Perhaps he did not come up with this thought; he could have been recording something he had heard elsewhere. Just the same, whether from his own thoughts or from something he had once heard, he wrote a profound truth about prayer.

About that same time my youngest child, fifteen years younger than his brother in DC, was in elementary school. That fall, as we drove home one afternoon from the Christian school he attended, he looked up at me from where he sat in the back seat and exclaimed with great enthusiasm, "Mom! Did you know God has a phone number?"

"God has a phone number?" I asked, peering back at him through my front mirror, perplexed by his words.

"Yes, He does!" my little boy answered as enthusiastic as ever. "We learned it at school today! It's Jeremiah 33:3!"

Stuck in stand-still carpool traffic, I quickly looked it up on my iPhone and found these words, "Call to me and I will answer you…."

"Yes, honey," I responded as a smile broke on my face. "God certainly does have a phone number!"

Prayer truly is the greatest privilege man can have. As Guerrant wrote in his journal, it moves the hand that moves the universe. Psalm 65:2 tells us that God hears our prayers, and Psalm 6:9 says He receives our prayers. And as my son claimed, He has a phone and we can call Him anytime, night or day, and we will never get a busy signal!

Prayer: Thank You, Lord, for letting us come to You any time we need to. Thank You that You hear and receive our prayer. Teach us to call out to You at all times—happy, sad, difficult, or joyous, in Jesus' name. Amen.

Ponder this: What a privilege to go to God about anything in prayer! Are you exercising your God-given privilege today?

Have Mercy, O Lord!
Read: 1 John 1:5-10

Then I acknowledged my sin to you and did not cover up my iniquity. I said 'I will confess my transgressions to the Lord.' And you forgave the guilt of my sin.

Psalm 32:5 (NIV)

What does confession of personal sin have to do with prayer? Everything! There is an abundance of Scripture that tells of the impact sin has on a person's prayer life. The Scriptures make two basic points. Godly living or personal holiness adds strength to our prayers, whereas sin detracts from them. These two points can be seen in many verses. The following are a few examples (all taken from the NIV):

- 1 Peter 4:7, "Therefore be alert and of sober mind so that you may pray…"
- Proverbs 15:29, "The LORD is far from the wicked, but he hears the prayer of the righteous."
- James 5:16, "Therefore confess your sins to each other and pray for each other so that you may be healed. The prayer of a righteous person is powerful and effective."
- 1 John 3:21, "Dear friends, if our hearts do not condemn us, we have confidence before God."
- Psalm 66:18, "If I had cherished sin in my heart, the LORD would not have listened."
- Isaiah 59:1-2, "Surely the arm of the LORD is not too

short to save, nor His ear too dull to hear; but your iniquities have separated you from your God; your sins have hidden His face from you, so that He will not hear."

So, what are we to do if we have sinned? Romans 3:10 tells us that we are all sinners. It says no one is righteous, not even one. Then, how can we hope to have God hear our prayers if we are not righteous? The answer to that is found in the cross. Jesus took our sins upon Him when He died on the cross, and if we believe in Him we take on His righteousness. This is why ongoing confession of our sins is so important—both for our own spiritual lives and for our prayer life. But the good news is: God is merciful and He faithfully forgives our sins when we confess them to Him in prayer.

Have you ever heard of the Mercy Seat of God? If you are like me, you have probably heard the term, though it seems like some vague and mysterious item that the Bible makes mention of, but you really have no idea what it is. At least that's how I felt about it for many years until one day when I was reading through the Psalms in my devotions and came across Psalm 80:1.

This verse says, "Hear us, Shepherd of Israel, you who led Joseph like a flock. You who sit enthroned between the cherubim shine forth." This verse gave me pause as I tried to imagine God's throne. I pictured a magnificent throne with cherubim on either side.

But then something gnawed at my subconscious. Where had I heard about the cherubim before? I had an inkling that they were mentioned in the Old Testament somewhere. Then it hit me—they are mentioned in the description of the Ark of the Covenant. I found this reference to cherubim in Exodus 25:17-18. In these verses, God instructs Moses regarding the construction of the Mercy Seat. It was to be made out of pure gold and two cherubim, also made of gold, were to be placed on either side of it. And of course, this was a physical representation of the real Mercy Seat which we cannot see with our human eyes.

That's when I realized something. Wow! The cherubim are on either side of the Mercy Seat! So, what is between the cherubim? The Mercy Seat! But what else is between the cherubim according to this verse in Psalms? The very throne of God! Is it possible that God's throne is on the Mercy Seat?

Yes, God is faithful and just to forgive all who ask Him. And to quote my pastor, Mark Janke, "When we come to God we are coming to the throne of grace, not the throne of merit." How wonderful to be able to bring our prayers, petitions, and praises to the very throne of God unencumbered by our sins if we only confess them and ask His forgiveness.

Prayer: Gracious Heavenly Father, thank You so much for the privilege of prayer. Thank You for forgiving our sins so freely. Please bring to our minds any unconfessed sins so that we may confess them to You and have a right relationship with You once more. Hear our prayers, O Lord, in Your Son's name. Amen.

Ponder this: God is in the business of forgiving sins, and He will forgive yours and mine if we will only confess them to Him. Then, we will be able to pray with more power. What do you need to ask forgiveness for today?

To God Be the Glory
Read: Psalm 29:1-9

Ascribe to the LORD the glory due His name;
worship the LORD in the splendor of His holiness.
Psalm 29:2 (NIV)

The country of my birth and blissful childhood is half a world away across a vast ocean. There's a name for people like me. We are called "Third-Culture Kids" or TCKs. We are a group of people who were born and/or raised in one country but have citizenship in another. Shirley is a TCK, too. She and I are both MKs, or missionary kids. I lived across a dirt road from Shirley when we were children in the town of Ogbomoso, Nigeria.

I spent the first ten years of my life in that tropical African country, a place I loved very much. When a war-ravaged this once beautiful place, my family returned to the United States. But, as a child, I spent seemingly endless summer-like days in Africa climbing trees and chasing lizards, eating guavas picked straight from the tree, and watching chameleons change color.

The rainy season in Nigeria is breath-taking. The once brown, dusty world suddenly becomes lush and green. There is no more beautiful place in the world than Nigeria during the rainy season. The daily rain washes everything new and sparkling clean, exposing green in various shades all around. I can remember the water drops glistening on the grass and leaves in the bright sun after one of the daily rain showers.

As an adult, I have traded those tropical scenes for bright fall foliage and days when the world is covered in a blanket of white snow, and I sit inside next to a fire warming-up my cold hands with hot chocolate.

When I think of God showing His glory, I think of it in nature—His handiwork. To David, the immense size of the firmament and the regularity of the planet's movement showed him God's glory. We see this in many places in Psalms such as in 19:1, when he wrote, "The heavens declare the glory of God; the skies proclaim the work of his hands." I can just picture him looking up at the stars on a clear night while he watched his sheep.

On the drive to school one morning, when my youngest son was a child, he suddenly said to me, "Hey Mom! Look! Those clouds look like the word 'Hi' in the sky." Truth be told, I was unable to see what my son was referring to because of my vantage point and the need to keep my eyes focused on the road ahead of me, so I asked him to explain. He pointed out the window next to his seat and said, "Well, there are a lot of straight lines in the clouds. Two are tall with a connecting puff between them and there is a smaller cloud beside them." I knew the sky had some streaks of cirrus clouds in it, so my son's explanation was believable. Then just as spontaneously, my son waved to the sky and offered a cheery and sincere, "Hi God!"

Do we take time to notice God in all His glory, in whatever ways He shows it? God takes His glory seriously. In Isaiah 42:8, He says He will not give His glory to another. And in other Old Testament passages, He showed His glory in profound ways—lightning, peals of thunder, and billows of smoke.

In the Psalms, we see prayers based on God's glory many times. To ask God to answer our prayers for His own sake, rather than ours, or to pray that He be glorified in whatever happens in our lives pleases Him. But God is also concerned with our good. When we pray, He works in our lives for His glory... and for our good.

Prayer: Heavenly Father, to You belong glory and honor and praise. Teach us to see Your handiwork all around us. Be glorified in our lives, in Jesus' name. Amen.

Ponder this: Have you noticed the glory of God in some way lately? What makes you stand in awe of God's glory?

God is Love
Read: Micah 7:18-20

Who is a God like you, who pardons iniquity and passes over the rebellious acts of the remnant of His possession? He does not retain His anger forever because He delights in unchanging love.
Micah 7:18 (NASB)

God delights in unchanging love. Are those beautiful words or what?

As I studied prayer, I noticed that petitions based on God's character traits are a common practice in the Bible. They make for powerful prayers, too. This basis for petitioning God can be seen over and over in the Bible. It runs like a common thread among so many of the prayers throughout Scripture. And just what are these traits? A study of Psalms reveals many of them. Let's review them.

Love: When I was a child, I learned a little jingle that I recited while also making hand motions. First, I held my hands together and then opened them, saying, "I open my Bible book and read, 'God is love.'" God's steadfast love is mentioned well over 100 times in the Psalms. It is mentioned more than any of God's other traits. It is as if, of all God's many traits, the one He wants us to remember Him by most is His love. This is what the Psalms say about God's love: It endures forever (Psalm 100:5). The Lord abounds in it (Psalm 86:15). It is higher than the heavens (Psalm 57:10). It is from everlasting to everlasting

(Psalm 103:17). It is better than life (Psalm 63:3). It is precious (Psalm 36:7). It is toward those who fear Him (Psalm 103:17). He will crown us with it (Psalm 103:4). He will not remove it (Psalm 89:33). He takes pleasure in those who hope in it (Psalm 147:11). He shows compassion because of it (Psalm 106:45).

Faithfulness: The character trait which is referred to in the Psalms the second greatest number of times is faithfulness. What the Psalms teach about God's faithfulness includes: God's work is done in faithfulness (Psalm 33:4). God abounds in faithfulness (Psalm 86:15); faithfulness surrounds God (Psalm 89:8); it goes before God (Psalm 89:14). God will not be false to His faithfulness (Psalm 89:33); it endures forever (Psalm 117:2); it preserves us (Psalm 40:11); it is a shield to us (Psalm 91:4).

There are so many other traits mentioned in the Psalms which are used as a basis for petitions. If you look for this as you read the Psalms, you will notice it. Here are just some of the other traits I found. God is a fortress, a stronghold, a shield, deliverer, and redeemer. He is full of goodness, mercy, graciousness. He does wondrous things, is slow to anger, shows compassion, and forgives our sins. He heals diseases, is the King of glory, strong and mighty, and is mighty in battle. He is near to us and strengthens our hearts. He is robed in majesty. He does not sleep or slumber. He heals the brokenhearted, is the upholder of life, and is abundant in power. His understanding is beyond measure. He takes pleasure in those who fear Him. He makes peace, is the father to the fatherless and the protector of widows. He will not forsake His people, and He is good. He feeds the hungry, lifts up those who are bowed down, and sets the prisoner free. He lives. His way is perfect, His words are true, and His gentleness makes us great. All of these can be found in the

Psalms, and there are others as well!

Think of how a lawyer presents his petitions before a judge. He does not ask for a favorable ruling simply because his client desires one. No, he bases his argument on the law. And certainly, he is far more likely to get a favorable ruling if he can show that the law backs up his request. Likewise, when coming before God with requests, if they are based on who God is and what He has promised then like a lawyer's argument based on the law, you can know your petitions are in good standing. This is one reason it is so powerful to pray the Scriptures. The Scriptures spell out who God is and what he has promised. The more we learn of God through His Word the stronger our prayers become.

Prayer: Oh Lord, You are so good to me. Thank You for pouring Your love upon me. You have so many wonderful traits which You demonstrate in my life and in Your Word. May my requests before You be in keeping with Your will and Your ways. Hear my prayers, O Lord, in Jesus' name. Amen.

Ponder this: God has so many wonderful traits. Get to know the God you serve better and better each day through prayer and Bible study.

I Am in Prayer
Read: Psalm 109:1-4

In return for my friendship they accuse me,
but I am a man of prayer.
Psalm 109:4 (NIV)

One of my favorite verses is the second half of Psalm 109:4. It simply says "...but I am a man of prayer." In the American Standard Bible, this verse reads, "...but I am in prayer." It's just five little words, but it says it all! What makes this statement so powerful is the context in which it appears. In the verses that precede it, David complains adamantly about his situation. He begs God not to be silent, telling God that he is being treated unfairly. People are lying about him. They encircle him with hate, they attack him without cause. In return for his love, they accuse him. They reward him evil for good and hatred for love. Then, after saying all of that, David writes "...but I am in prayer." It seems that in David's mind, the strongest weapon he had against his enemies was prayer.

Though grown now, my youngest son, Ty, had a robotic, battery-operated, tyrannosaurus rex toy as a child. When turned on, the large, scary-looking dinosaur would move around in a slow, stalking manner and growl. Its motions were jerky and intimidating. Its feet and hands had large claws, and when it growled, it opened its mouth, showing off a set of sharp teeth. After Ty outgrew this toy, we kept it in the basement along with other toys for my grandson, Grason, to play with.

When Grason was only two years old, Ty brought the dinosaur out of the toy box, set it near Grason, and turned it on to see his reaction. (Had I known Ty was doing this, I probably would not have allowed it. At only two years old, little Grason would almost certainly be frightened by the toy). It did frighten Grason, but instead of crying or running away, he stood up from where he had been sitting, straightened his back with a determined air about him, and looked intently at the dinosaur.

Then the toy monster moved its feet, causing it to take a step closer to Grason. As it moved, it opened his scary mouth and growled. By this time, I had heard the growl and had run into the room in time to observe Grason's actions. He walked very slowly away from the toy, keeping his eye firmly fixed upon it. Then he picked up a miniature wooden baseball bat that had been lying on the floor nearby. With the bat securely in his hands, he walked cautiously back toward the toy. He stood very still right in front of the toy, moved his hand back into a swing stance and then gave the menacing tyrannosaurus rex a hard blow with the bat! All of us in the room burst out laughing and then Ty turned the toy off and declared Grason the winner, telling him he had defeated the scary monster!

How do you respond when faced with frightening or challenging circumstances? Do you run and hide? Do you freeze in fear, or feel overwhelmed with panic? Or, like Grason, do you attack the problem?

What did David do? David prayed. David's choice of action against the strong and wicked forces that opposed him was the same choice of action we can take in whatever frightening or difficult circumstances we find ourselves. This truth has been a great comfort to me in difficulties I have faced, especially when it feels like there is nothing I can do about the problem. There is always something I can do. I can pray. Yes, I can always pray, and from this passage, it appears that prayer is a strong weapon for fighting life's battles—much better than a miniature wooden bat (or any other solution we might come up with on our own.)

"...but I am in prayer."

Prayer: Father, what a privilege it is to pray! Your Word teaches us that prayer is powerful and brings about real changes. Lord, You are strong and mighty and able to help us with our needs. Thank You for hearing our prayers, in Jesus' name. Amen.

Ponder this: Prayer is powerful! What battle—spiritual or physical—do you have in your life right now? Are you using the powerful spiritual weapon of prayer to fight it?

Chapter Three

Prayer Lessons from Paul

Shirley

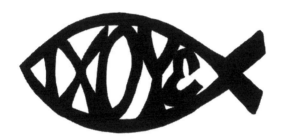

An Extraordinary Encounter
Read: Acts 9:1-9

Therefore, if anyone is in Christ, he is a new creation; old things have passed away; behold, all things have become new.
2 Corinthians 5:17 (NKJV)

When my parents were missionaries in Nigeria, my dad rode a motorcycle to remote villages that could not be reached by car. His interpreter would hold Dad's accordion and hang on for dear life! When they arrived at a village, he and his interpreter would find a big tree under which Dad could stand, out of the direct sun while he preached. To gather a crowd so he could preach to them, Dad would pull out his accordion and play upbeat music. The Nigerian people love music with a beat and would gather to see what was going on. Once a crowd gathered, he'd begin to preach the gospel.

At one village, as he was preaching, a very old little woman started coming toward him speaking loudly and excitedly to him in a voice that my dad interpreted as angry. She motioned for him to follow her. The interpreter told him she wanted to show him something. She took him to the center of the village where the idol hut was located. As it turned out, she was the priestess who cared for the idols and offered the idols' sacrifices for all of her people.

She grabbed a club that my dad thought she was going to use on him and began hitting and destroying all of the idols. As she destroyed the idols she said through the interpreter, "I always knew there was a God who loved me and who I didn't have to be afraid of!"

The change in this woman was instant and complete. It was indeed extraordinary. She went from protecting and caring for the idols to totally destroying them.

Today's passage describes another extraordinary encounter with God. The persecutor and killer of Christ-followers, Saul, was traveling to Damascus to find men and women who were followers of Christ on whom he could unleash his anger as he beat, imprisoned, and killed them. While on the road to Damascus, Saul had an extraordinary encounter with Jesus that resulted in a spectacular transformation: from Saul the persecutor and killer of Christ-followers to Paul an Apostle of Jesus Christ (1 Timothy 1:1). In the Bible, God changed the name of some individuals to serve as a reminder that they were not who they used to be—they had been transformed!

Many call Paul the greatest preacher in the Christian church. After conversion, he fervently shared the gospel and made disciple-makers. And, he authored (under the inspiration of the Holy Spirit) many of the New Testament books of the Bible.

God is in the business of total transformation. Regardless of your horrific and sinful past, God is able to transform you into a new creation as we see in our focal passage. This transformation refers to the new creation that is the result of salvation.

Colossians 1:21 also speaks of transformation that leads to reconciliation in Christ as we read, "And you, who once were alienated and enemies in your mind by wicked works, yet now He has reconciled" (NKJV). In this verse, Paul is speaking to Christ-followers reminding them to be continually transformed by the gospel through the power of the Holy Spirit.

Prayer: God, thank You for how You are transforming me by renewing my mind through Your Holy Spirit-inspired Word. Help me to trust You and not block the work of Your Spirit in my life, in Jesus' name. Amen.

Ponder this: Have you been transformed by an extraordinary encounter with the living God? In what ways would you like for God to transform you? In what ways does God want to transform you? What things are blocking the transforming work of Christ in your life?

Chief of All Sinners
Read: 1 Timothy 1:12-17

This is a faithful saying and worthy of all acceptance, that Christ Jesus came into the world to save sinners, of whom I am chief.
1 Timothy 1:15 (NKJV)

When I was a teenager, my dad founded and directed a drug rehabilitation program. Often in the early days of the program before the residential center was open, my brother Tim or I would be moved out of our beds so one of the addicts could have a comfortable bed and a place to detox.

The gospel was at the center of any help my dad gave. Time and time again I would hear one of these young men or women, who had sunk deeply into the addiction lifestyle and all that it entailed, say, "I have to get cleaned up and straightened out, and then I can come to Jesus." Or, they would recount all the horribly sinful things they had done and explain, "There is no way God would even consider forgiving me."

I learned well from the patient, loving, methodical way that my dad, and mom, would explain the gospel to them over and over.

These young men and women did not understand that they could do nothing to get good enough or earn God's forgiveness; that it is only God's grace through the sacrifice of His Son that can bring forgiveness of our sin.

Paul's statement in today's focal passage stands in stark

contrast to the statements of these young men and women. Paul makes a confident declaration that Jesus Christ "came into the world to save sinners," and follows this with a confession that he is chief among sinners.

Let's go back to the time before Paul's conversion when he was called Saul and his mission in life was to persecute Christians—a job at which he excelled! His reputation was extensive and the Christ-following community feared him.

When Paul encountered Jesus on the road to Damascus, he was totally transformed. His mission changed completely, for instead of persecuting and killing Christians, he now told others about Jesus Christ and was a wonderful disciple-maker.

So, why did Paul call himself the chief among all sinners? Because, Paul grew in his understanding of God's characteristics—who God is—he grew in his awareness of the grievousness of his own sin. As Paul understood that God's holiness is the standard, he called himself the chief of all sinners in a humble expression of how far short he was of meeting God's standard.

What can we learn from Paul's confession? The clearer our understanding of who God is in His God-ness, the clearer our understanding will be of the presence and magnitude of our own sin. An honest recognition of my need for the Savior enables me to focus on God's mercy and grace to me and not to wrongly dwell on my sinfulness. And, our salvation expresses itself humbly.

The contrast in the responses of the young men and women at the addiction center and Paul is stark. One expresses that his sin is so great God cannot forgive him. Paul expresses that because Christ is so great, He is able to save sinners, so that mercy and grace abound toward him as he is forgiven for his many sins.

Prayer: Father, help me know You as I read, study, memorize, meditate upon and contemplate Your Word. By Your Holy Spirit, enable me to recognize the depth of my sin, and be quick to confess and repent of that sin, as I walk in the freedom of Your forgiveness. In Your Son's name, I pray. Amen.

Ponder this: As we learn more about who God is, we cannot help but recognize how far short of God's standard of holiness we fall. There is a fine line between recognizing our sinfulness and focusing on our sinfulness. As you become more aware of your sinfulness, focus on God's mercy and grace in your life.

This is My Prayer
Read: Philippians 1:3-11

And this is my prayer…
Philippians 1:9-11 (NIV)

I have had a myriad of opportunities to learn how to pray throughout my life. My parents, family, Nigeria mission family, and countless Christ-followers in Nigeria and the United States have taught and shown me how to pray in the midst of various life situations. And, I have been honored to have so many godly men and women pray for me throughout my life.

What are some of the things for which people have prayed for me? Some prayed that I would come to a saving knowledge of Jesus Christ. Many prayed for God's mercy to spare my life and restore my health when I was seriously ill because of a dead kidney and infection running rampant throughout my body. Many have prayed for me as I have made decisions about job changes. Countless people prayed for me as I grieved the deaths of my dad, mom, two brothers, a nephew, and many other family members and friends.

These are just a few of the prayers people prayed for me that also taught me how to pray for others.

I have learned so much from the prayers of these godly men and women whom God brought into my life. When my dad would encounter someone for whom he had been praying, he always would say, "This is how I am praying."

So now, when someone asks me to pray about a situation, I usually tell them, "I will be praying that…" And, like my dad, when I speak with them again or write them a note, I tell them "I have been praying…"

Paul, in today's focal passage, is telling the Christ-followers in Philippi, "This is my prayer" for you, and then he tells them how and for what he was praying. He was praying for the spiritual growth of those whom he loved. It was his passion to not only share the gospel with unbelievers, but to make disciple-makers who were growing in their faith by studying and learning the Word of God, praying, and being diligent to obey and practice what they were learning. Paul continued praying that they would bear the fruit of righteousness which is the result of abiding in Christ.

Basically, Paul prayed that we would do our part in reading, studying, memorizing, meditating upon, and contemplating the Word of God as we stand ready to obey the Word and, by God's grace, be transformed into the image of Christ—the goal of sanctification.

I imagine that the knowledge of how Paul was praying for them encouraged the Philippians to continue growing in their faith.

In this prayer, Paul reminds us to focus on the spiritual needs of those for whom we pray. That does not mean that we should not pray for physical needs to be met as Jesus taught us in the Model Prayer (Luke 11:1-4). It means that we should pray for the associated spiritual needs of the person in addition to praying for their physical needs to be met or for physical healing.

Prayer: Heavenly Father, thank You for the many examples in

Scripture and in our lives of how and for what to pray. Give me a passion to pray more consistently and fervently. Make me more aware of how to pray for others, in Jesus' name. Amen.

Ponder this: Who has prayed for you throughout your life and for what have they prayed? Have you been encouraged by hearing how and for what someone has prayed for you? For whom are you praying, and how are you praying for them? In what ways can you become more aware of the needs of others?

Devote Yourself to Prayer
Read: Colossians 4:2-6

Devote yourselves to prayer, being watchful and thankful.
Colossians 4:2 (NIV)

Have you ever known someone who devoted themselves to prayer? I have known a few throughout my life. One in particular that comes to mind was a dear widow who was blind. She would tell people, "There are many things I cannot do, but I can sit at home and pray!" And that is precisely what she did. She prayed for each of her family members, for her church family, and for her neighbors and their families. She would listen to the news to know how she needed to pray for leaders, people and situations locally, statewide, nationally, and worldwide.

She would call the church office to ask if anyone was in the hospital, sick, or in need of prayer. She prayed diligently for my dad (her pastor), my mom, and our entire family. She truly devoted herself to prayer.

The whole Bible makes it clear that God wants us to pray confessing our sins, asking Him for our needs and desires, and giving Him thanks. Prayer is a Christ-follower exercising his or her faith in God's God-ness. Implied in our prayers is trusting God to answer them according to His will.

Devoting yourself to prayer means that prayer is a priority in your life. You don't just squeeze it in when you have a little extra time, or when there is nowhere else you can turn. We are also told that we are to be watchful or alert. That means we are to pay attention to the things going on around us. Is a co-worker or Sunday school class member sick or discouraged? Has that young couple not been at church in several weeks? Is that teenager no longer involved in youth group?

My mom had a dedicated season of prayer in the morning. When she ended her time of morning praying she would say, "I pray these things according to your will, Lord." She wouldn't say, "Amen," the way so many of us end our prayers.

Why? Because she hadn't ended her prayer. That dedicated season of prayer in the morning prepared her heart and mind and opened the way for those ongoing conversations with God throughout her day as she prayed about things that came to her mind and gave thanks to God for His provision. Her attitude of prayer made her alert to those around her who needed prayer.

Then, each night before she went to sleep she had another dedicated season of prayer, not just a "God bless so and so," but a thoughtful time of intercession. That night prayer would end with her, "Amen," and she would go to sleep.

What does it mean to be devoted to prayer? It means that you don't just pray here and there, but you make seasons of prayer a priority in your life. You don't lie in bed at the end of a long day and try to stay awake long enough to pray.

Like my mom, we have to learn to pray, and part of that learning is to schedule our prayer times and make them a priority. Once we begin praying, we will desire more and more to communicate through prayer with our Heavenly Father.

As Christ-followers we must be diligent to read, study, memorize, meditate upon, and contemplate the Holy Spirit-inspired Word of God; and as we learn to pray, we will learn to devote ourselves to prayer.

Prayer: Our Heavenly Father, thank You for inviting us to pray to You, and for desiring that we communicate our deepest heartfelt thoughts, fears, and desires to You. We thank You for the grace, mercy, love, and strength we receive when we pray. In the name of Your Son Jesus, we pray. Amen.

Ponder this: What changes would you have to make in your life in order to devote yourself to prayer? How can you prepare your heart to pray? Are you alert throughout the day so that you recognize those around you in need of the Savior? Do you exhibit an attitude of thanksgiving in and through your life and your prayers?

Day 5

The No's of God
Read: 2 Corinthians 12:7-10

But he said to me, "My grace is sufficient for you,
for my power is made perfect in weakness."
Therefore, I will boast all the more gladly about my weaknesses,
so that Christ's power may rest on me.
2 Corinthians 12:9 (NIV)

Throughout my life, the Lord has said no to many of my prayers. Admittedly, at the time He said no I was not always thrilled with His response. As you read the following accounts of God saying no to my prayers, keep in mind that I didn't always pray, "…according to Your will, God."

I remember praying that a friend would fully recover from a car accident and be allowed to raise her infant son. God said no.

I prayed for the Lord to open a position for me at a particular company where I wanted to work. God said no.

I prayed that the cancer treatment for my friend would do its job and eradicate the cancer from her body. God said no, and the cancer spread instead, leading to her death.

I prayed that the Lord would allow a relationship to continue flourishing as we were heading toward marriage. God said no.

It is a fact that sometimes God says no to our prayer requests. There are many other instances when my prayers were answered with no, just as I know there are also many such instances in your prayer life. I would like to tell you that in each instance when God said no I responded with understanding, trusting Him in everything, but I didn't.

Because of the amount of time that has passed since God said no to some of my prayers, I can look back upon many of these times with a different perspective and see the blessing of God's protection and provision through His no.

The no's often helped me recognize and trust God's power in my weakness. At times, because the no left me at my wits' end, it sent me running to God for safety and rest. God's no's helped me learn to depend upon Him for everything!

In every instance, I am confident that the Lord used the no to sanctify me, meaning that He answered the prayer according to His will for me, which ultimately made me more into His image. God, through His Holy Spirit-inspired Word, has taught me who He is, thus enabling me to trust Him and His purposes more fully.

From the times that God said no to the prayers for my friends, I have learned to be a better listener, which enables me to pray more effectively for others. I have also learned to be more kind and gentle in my care for them, and I have seen the power of God strengthen His people to withstand spiritual attacks and the attacks of debilitating disease.

The no's in life have led me to continually do several things:

Ask the Lord to make me aware of any unconfessed sin in my life so I would be quick to confess and repent of that sin, and walk in the freedom of His forgiveness.

Pray for strength to trust Him as I walk through the situation.

And, to ask God to help me "lay aside the old self... be renewed in the spirit of (my) mind, and put on the new self" (Ephesians 4:22-24 NKJV). God's no's send me to His Word to reinforce and renew the truth about who God is.

In today's passage, we read about the Apostle Paul praying three times for the Lord to remove a thorn in his flesh, but God said no to Paul's request.

Paul said the Lord told him, "My grace is sufficient for you, for my power is made perfect in weakness."

Paul also told us in Philippians 4:19, "And my God will supply all of your need according to His riches in glory by Christ Jesus" (KJV).

These two passages teach us that when God says no to our request, His grace will carry us through, and, God will supply our every spiritual need as His power is manifested because of our weakness.

When God says no He brings about His will in our lives which sanctifies us more and more. These no's send us to the Bible so we can know Him better and trust Him more. Sometimes through the no's, we become more aware of sin in our hearts as we see the selfishness of our prayers. Other times, it seems that the no's are reminders to me that I need more of Jesus, not other people or things.

Prayer: Father, help me to trust and rest in Your sufficient grace at all times, particularly when You say no to my prayers. Help me to recognize my need for Your grace all the time. In the name of Jesus, I pray. Amen.

Ponder this: All we bring to our relationship with God is our weakness; God brings His all-sufficient grace. How have you grown in your relationship with God through His no's?

Chapter Four
Meditations from Moses' Life

Harriet

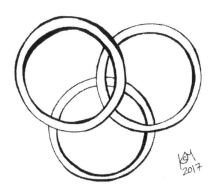

Who, Me?
Read: Exodus 3:11-12, Amos 7:14- 15

But Moses said to God, "Who am I that I should go to Pharaoh
and bring the Israelites out of Egypt?"
Exodus 3:11 (NIV)

"Who, me? God, you can't possibly be asking me to do that! I'm not capable."

Have you ever said something like that to God? What have you sensed God asking you to do that made you think perhaps He had asked the wrong person?

Moses felt this way when he heard God speaking to him from a burning bush. God told Moses he had been chosen for a special job. God had seen the affliction of His people in Egypt and would deliver them using Moses as the instrument for delivery. He instructed Moses to go to Pharaoh and bring His people out of their captivity in Egypt. And what was Moses's reaction? He gave every excuse he could think of to try and convince God that he was not the right person for the job. He practically begged God to find someone else.

Amos did something similar. In Amos 7:14-15, when a man named Amaziah accused him of being a prophet, Amos answered, "I was neither a prophet nor the son of a prophet, but I was a shepherd, and I also took care of sycamore-fig trees."

Every now and then a verse of Scripture strikes me as a little bit humorous. This verse struck me that way the first time I read it. In this verse, the prophet Amos tells Amaziah that he's not a prophet, nor the son of a prophet. Amos claims to be nothing more than a herdsman and a grower of sycamore trees. I think Amos's comment is funny, perhaps because I can relate to it so well. How many times have I perceived God asking me to do something for Him, whether it was to go on a mission trip, write a devotional, or teach a Sunday school class, when I have told God, "But God, I am not a teacher or the daughter of a teacher… I am just a housewife and a grower of tomato bushes!"

But Amos did become a prophet and Moses also became a mighty leader who led God's people out of captivity. How did this transformation occur? God did it, of course, but it started with these men communing with God. It started with prayer.

God is not offended when we tell him about our fears and reservations. 1 Peter 5:7 tells us to cast all our cares on God because He cares for us. My sister reminded my father of this verse once when we were children in Africa. We lived there in a time of war and great turmoil. On this particular occasion, we had heard rumors that an angry mob was attacking the king of our little town. We occupied the mission house closest to the town, in fact, its driveway exited onto the town's main road.

Because of the impending threat, my parents hurriedly tried to pack-up and move us in with another missionary family farther away from the town. My parent's nerves were shot. But my sister, about eight years old at the time, pranced around them, completely carefree, dancing and whistling. My father spoke to her rather sharply saying, "Alisa, don't you understand the danger we are in?"

Alisa looked up at him in her childlike innocence and answered, "But Daddy, I heard you preach last Sunday, and you told us to cast all our cares on God because God cares for us."

Talk about "out of the mouths of babes!"

As it turned out, the mob did attack the king. They killed him and dragged his dead body down that main road right in front of our house. But we were safe and so were our home and property. The riot settled down in a few short days, a new king was crowned, and we moved back into our house and returned to our normal lives.

I think about these things, and I know my parents must have felt inadequate many times as they served God in a foreign land. I, too, have felt that sense of inadequacy at times, like when God first laid it on my heart to be a writer. But here we are— missionaries, writers, prophets, and leaders. We are far more than just growers of sycamore trees and tomato plants… and it all starts with prayer.

Prayer: Father, You are a caring God. You are not bothered by our feelings of inadequacy. You use us for Your glory in ways we could never have imagined in spite of our doubts. Teach us to cast our cares on You, in Jesus' name. Amen.

Ponder this: Who, me? I can't! Have you said this about a situation lately? God answers back, "Yes, you, and yes, you can!"

God's Blessings or God?
Read: Exodus 33:1-3, 15

Then Moses said to him, "If your Presence does not go with us,
do not send us up from here,"
Exodus 33:15 (NIV)

"Hi, Mom! Hi Dad! I'm glad you're home—what did you bring me?"

How many times have we heard our kids welcome us home like that? Or for that matter, how many times have we welcomed our parents that way? I can remember wanting to see what my parents brought me from a trip while taking my parents' safe return home for granted.

Have you ever given a gift to someone and felt like he or she was more interested in the gift than in you? Or, let's put the shoe on the other foot; have you ever been guilty yourself of being more excited about a gift than about the person who gave it to you? I think we often treat God this way. We long for His blessings in our lives, but do we long for Him? When we pray, we ask Him to bless us, and we bring a long list of suggested ways for Him to do just that. We hope He says yes to all of our many requests and lavishes abundant blessings upon us and upon those we love. Yet, we often don't even slow down our busy lives enough to spend time with Him or to truly worship Him.

Moses was a great intercessor. As he led the Israelites out of bondage and into the Promised Land, he interacted with God many times, intervening between the children of Israel and God. And Moses wanted God more than the blessings God could provide. How do I know this?

Today's verse gives insight into Moses's heart. This passage comes right after a time when the children of Israel had been quite rebellious. Do you remember the story of the golden calf? While Moses was on Mount Sinai receiving the Ten Commandments from God, the people grew tired of waiting for his return. They wanted something to worship, so they made the image of a calf out of gold and they worshiped this image instead of worshiping God. This provoked God's anger against the people. Because of His anger, although He agreed to allow them to continue going to the Promised Land as He had already said He would, He added that He would not go with them.

But God promised His blessings. He said He would send His angel ahead of Moses and the people and drive out all of their enemies—the Canaanites, the Amorites, the Hittites, the Perizzites, the Hivites, and the Jebusites. He said He would let the people enter that land for which they so longed, and which He had promised to them—the land flowing with milk and honey. God was offering not just His blessings, but His abundant blessings—however, not His presence.

How did Moses respond?

Moses refused to accept God's blessings without His presence. What a glimpse into Moses's heart! He loved God so much that he truly desired God's presence more than His blessings. He knew what all of us should know; without God's presence and His abiding Spirit, everything else is worthless. We see this in Moses's answer. He told God that if God's presence would not go with them, then he didn't want God to even allow them to get to the Promised Land, no matter how easy the journey and how wonderful the land might be once there.

In Matthew 22:37 (NIV), Jesus identified the greatest of all the commandments when He said, "Love the Lord your God with all your heart and with all your soul and with all your mind." Moses exemplified this. I have to ask myself, do I practice this greatest commandment?

When I think of it back in earthly terms, and think about my parents, I realize what a treasure it is to still have them living, even as they are aging and have lived longer than many of their friends. From this perspective, I can easily see how much better it is to love the person rather than the object. But do I do that with God?

When I'm having my quiet time and praying to God, am I using it as an opportunity to just seek blessings from Him, or am I enjoying His company? Am I only making petitions to God, or do some of my prayers include praises and thanksgiving? Am I thinking only of my requests, or am I spending some of the time remembering who He is and that He is worthy to be worshiped simply because He is God, regardless of how happy or comfortable I may be at that moment?

Prayer: Oh, how You have blessed us, O Lord! Make us ever mindful of Your tender love toward us and Your compassion upon us. Draw us near that we may love You more. May we long for Your presence more than Your blessings; for You more than what You can do for us, in Jesus' name. Amen.

Ponder this: Which do you yearn for? What kinds of things do you ask God for? Are you desiring God or His blessings?

Carry Others' Burdens
Read: Numbers 11:10-17

Carry each other's burdens, and in this way
you fulfill the law of Christ.
Galatians 6:2 (NIV)

My father had a physically handicapped brother who was ten years his senior. Ben, his brother, started life out as a normal baby. And except for one winter when he had mumps, measles, and whooping cough all at the same time, his childhood also seemed unremarkable and normal in every way.

However, in late childhood, Ben began to have trouble walking. His problem became increasingly worse with the passing of each year. By the time he was in college, mobility had become such a problem that he fell a few times trying to walk to class. Other times he missed class altogether because walking on those mornings was just too difficult for him. He died suddenly from heart failure when he was only in his early twenties.

I have heard my father speak lovingly of his older brother, whom I never knew. My dad proudly told me once how in one college class, Ben's professor threw away the lowest grade for each of his pupils because the class seemed to be struggling so. For Ben, he threw away a 100 because Ben had nothing lower. My dad became a doctor and often speculated about what Ben might have had that caused his progressive decline and ultimate death and how things might have been different for Ben if he had lived today instead of in the 1940s.

When I was a teenager, there was a popular song on the radio about someone not being heavy because he was a brother. My dad loved that song. I still remember him hearing it on the radio with me in the car and seeing tears mist his eyes as he told me once again about his brother. Daddy told me of a time when Ben sat at a movie theater and laughed so hard he fell out of his seat into the aisle. Daddy tried to pull him up but was not strong enough. He was going to go get help but Ben said to wait until after the movie ended. And, Ben sat happily on the floor for the duration of the movie. Dad said he often let Ben lean on him to walk places and he spoke of how people would ask how such a little boy could shoulder someone ten years older.

My dad did not mind the physical burden of his brother Ben. Moses had a very different reaction to bearing other people's burdens. To be fair to Moses, he bore others' burdens many, many times without complaint. He loved the people under his care so much that he was willing to die with them in the wilderness rather than abandon the job God had given him. But, in today's passage, in Numbers 11, Moses seems to have reached his wit's end.

In verses 11 and 12, Moses asked God, "Why have you laid the burden of these people on me? Did I conceive them? Did I give birth to them that You should tell me to carry them around in my bosom like a nurse carries a child?"

This passage does not spotlight an example to follow in Moses's reactions to the stress of the day, as much as it spotlights God's gracious answer to Moses, and thus to us when we are at the end of our rope and come to Him. God didn't reprimand Moses for his lack of willingness to continue to carry the emotional burden of others. No, instead, God answered Moses's prayer by giving him help in his role of burden carrier.

In verse 16 and 17 of Numbers 11, God instructed Moses to select seventy men who would help to carry the people's burden so Moses wouldn't have to carry it alone. In verse 17 God tells Moses, "I will come down and speak with you there, and I will take some of the power of the Spirit that is on you and put it on them. They will share the burden of the people with you so that you will not have to carry it alone."

Whose burden is God asking you to carry today? Carrying one another's burdens is something God has called His people to do. This can be accomplished in many ways. Perhaps God wants you to share what you have with someone, contribute financially to her or her ministry, or maybe it's a visit that will help to lighten her burden. Or maybe, like me, God is calling you to faithfully lift her and her situation up in prayer. Ask God to show you whose burden He wants you to help carry and how best to do that.

Prayer: Heavenly Father, thank You for placing burdens on the hearts of Your people. Thank You for the way You lay the burdens of others on our hearts and our burdens on the hearts of others. Make us willing vessels for Your work, in Jesus' name. Amen.

Ponder this: Is God whispering to you about another person's needs? What burdens has He placed on your heart? What will you do about them?

Day 4
God is Able
Read: Exodus 32:9, 34:9

Our God is in heaven; he does whatever pleases him.
Psalm 115:2-4 (NIV)

If we have spent much time in church, we've probably all heard the expression, "God is able." But what is He able to do? Is He able to answer your heartfelt prayers?

The answer to that question is a resounding yes! However, if we are honest with ourselves we'd have to admit that it sometimes doesn't feel like He is answering them. I remember such a time many years ago. One of my children had grown into a rebellious young adult. He had walked away from the church and the beliefs his father and I had taught him when he was a child. At that particular time, he was grown and living many miles away from home. I felt like all was lost.

That year, I was studying the life of Moses in a group Bible study and came across today's passages. I can still remember sitting in a church pew and hearing my Bible study leader discussing these chapters in Exodus. First, she pointed to Exodus 32:9, where God told Moses that He had seen the people and knew they were obstinate. Then she read Exodus 34:9, where Moses pleaded with God on behalf of the people asking God to forgive their sins and make them His possession anyway, even though they were obstinate. My leader pointed out what a great leader Moses was and how much he cared for the people—but that's not what made the biggest impact on me that night.

As I listened to those passages, my heart cried out, "Can a person really pray that way, Lord? Can I pray that way for my child? Instead of waiting for him to have a change of heart and despairing that he never will, can I just ask You to forgive him and make him one of Your own anyway, in spite of himself?" As I thought about this, my heart took flight. If Moses prayed that way for the people he cared for, then so could I!

Though I didn't see any indication God was answering that prayer for a very long time, I just kept praying that prayer for my child. Praying that way always filled me with hope and confidence. I was not sure if God would answer my prayer, but just knowing that He could answer it reassured me and gave me reason to hope and rejoice. It also motivated me to keep praying for my child. Finally, about ten years later when I least expected it, God did exactly what I had asked of Him for so long. He turned my son's life around and put a new heart in him.

Seeing my wayward child turn back to God was no small miracle to me. God might just as well have moved a mountain in my backyard—that's how impossible my prayer request seemed all those years. I kept praying it anyway… and God answered.

We serve a powerful God who listens to the prayers of His people. We serve a God who is able indeed! The Bible makes this truth abundantly clear, over and over. Here are just a few examples of what God is able to do:

- He is able to make his people stand strong. – Romans 14:4
- He is able to subdue all things unto Himself. – Philippians 3:21
- He is able to keep what has been entrusted to Him. –

2 Timothy 1:12

♦ He is able to help those who are tempted. – Hebrews 2:18

♦ He is able to save to the uttermost those who draw near to God through Christ Jesus. – Hebrews 7:25

And in the book of Revelation, we see the Apostle John weeping because there was no one in Heaven or on earth who was found worthy to open the book and its seals. But, then one of the twenty-four elders from around God's throne tells him not to weep because the Lion from the tribe of Judah, the Root of David, is worthy and able to open the books.

Yes, God is able to do all things, some of which we've seen in the passages above. He can be trusted with our heartfelt prayer requests.

Prayer: Heavenly Father, we acknowledge Your omnipotence. We bow before You and come humbly into Your presence. We thank You for loving us, for sending Your son to die for us that we may have a relationship with You. And, we thank You for hearing our prayers and using Your great power to help us when we cry out to You, in Jesus' name. Amen.

Ponder this: God can do anything! What audacious prayer are you longing to bring to Him? Do you find yourself doubting His ability to answer? Bring that prayer to Him today!

Love Your Neighbor
Read: Numbers 27:12-18

And the second is like it; "Love your neighbor as yourself."
Matthew 22:38 (NIV)

When my parents came back to America after serving twelve years as missionaries in Nigeria, they settled in a small town in West Virginia. One afternoon, our doorbell rang. I answered the door and a kind, elderly woman handed me a cake and welcomed me to our new town. She gave her name and said she was from the church we had visited the week before.

Later that afternoon, when my mother returned home from shopping, she asked who had brought the cake. "Hmm… I can't remember her name exactly but I think it was something like Mrs. A-E," I answered. "She said she was from the church we visited last week."

"Oh, it must have been Mrs. Easley. She is a good friend of ours," Mom replied.

"No, that doesn't sound exactly right," I responded, but to no avail. My mother proceeded to call Mrs. Easley and thank her for the cake, only to find out that Mrs. Easley had not sent it. As it turned out, a woman named Mrs. Agee had given us the cake, but Mrs. Easley brought us a pie shortly after my mother's phone call. We have laughed about that mix-up for years!

Reaching out to a new neighbor or church member is certainly one way to love your neighbor, but there are many more. Moses loved his neighbors in many ways, not the least of which were all the prayers he lifted up on their behalf. Today's passage records one of the most precious intercessions for others that Moses ever made. In this passage, God allowed Moses to see the Promised Land but refused to allow him to enter it because of the way Moses had rebelled at the waters of Meribah.

How do you think Moses reacted to the disappointing, and perhaps devastating, reminder that he would never be allowed to enter the land? Moses had spent his adult life in search of this land. Yet, now, after all he had done to lead the people to the Promised Land, he would not be allowed to enter. How would you react to a situation such as this?

Was Moses angry, sad, or filled with self-pity? Did he defend himself before God? Did he argue that he should be allowed to enter? Did he claim that he deserved this as a reward for all his hard work? Did he resent God?

No, Moses did not react in any of the ways one might think he would. He reacted with deep concern for the people—his neighbors. He asked God to appoint someone to lead them in his place so that the people of the Lord would not be as a sheep without a shepherd. At a time when Moses experienced one of the greatest disappointments of his life, he was still more concerned with the needs of others than with his own. I have to ask myself, how do I love my neighbor? How often do I pray for them?

In Matthew 22:36 we read these words, "'Teacher, which is the greatest commandment in the Law?' Jesus replied, 'Love the Lord your God with all your soul and with all your mind.' This is the first and greatest commandment. And the second is like it; 'Love your neighbor as yourself.' All the Law and Prophets hang on these two commandments" (NIV).

We saw in a previous devotion how Moses exemplified the greatest commandment when he wanted God's presence more than His blessings. Now we see that Moses also exemplified the second greatest commandment when he was truly more concerned with the needs of others than with his own disappointment.

Do we love God more than anything else in our lives? Do we spend time meditating on His Word and worshiping Him? Do we love others as much as we love ourselves?

Prayer: Oh Lord, we confess our shortcomings to You. We are self-centered creatures who have trouble really caring about others. Please also give us genuine love for them. Thank You for giving us the example of Moses to see how it should be, in Jesus' name. Amen.

Ponder this: Do we really love others? Think about the people you encountered today or in the last few days. Did you feel love for them? Did you see their side, situation, or need as well as you saw your own?

Chapter Five
Call on God

Shirley

To Save Unbelievers
Read: 2 Timothy 2:25-26

Brethren, my heart's desire and prayer to God for them
is that they may be saved.
Romans 10:1 (NASB)

A lady who was new to the church my dad pastored showed up at our kitchen door one Friday evening, just as Mom and I were heading out to the grocery store. She was in her mid-twenties and had come to Christ a couple of years after she married. Her husband was not a Christ-follower.

The lady told Mom she just needed to talk, so Mom told her to get in the car with us and go to the grocery store. The woman told Mom she was having a particularly difficult time understanding why God would not go ahead and save her husband. As usual, Mom listened patiently.

We arrived at the grocery store, went in and got a cart, and started shopping. We began in the produce section. Mom was not pleased with the green tomatoes, so she called for the produce manager to ask if there were more tomatoes in the back.

We were several aisles over from the produce section by the time the manager found us. He explained he didn't have any tomatoes that were as ripe as Mom wanted, but he expected a produce delivery the next day and thought Mom would find suitable tomatoes among those.

Mom asked if he would put aside one large basket of ripe

tomatoes for her to get the next morning around ten. He said he would be glad to, so we finished shopping.

When we got the groceries and ourselves in the car, the lady looked at Mom and said, "Jeannie! I can't believe that you had the nerve to ask him to find you ripe tomatoes in the back. And when you asked him to gather you a basket of ripe tomatoes to pick up in the morning, I thought I would die of embarrassment! How could you do that?"

Mom pulled the car back into the parking space from which she was backing out, put the car in park, and turned face-to-face with the lady.

"Why wouldn't I ask the produce manager to help me find what I want? That's what he is there for. I'm a good customer, and he always helps me find what I'm looking for."

As Mom spoke about the produce manager, I knew from the look on her face and the tone of her voice that in just seconds she would be talking about praying to God.

Mom began to ask the lady if she had been praying for God to save her husband. The lady said that she had prayed that a couple of times. Mom shot me a look that told me I was not to make a sound.

In the following minutes, Mom taught this woman that Father God delights in His children praying to Him. She explained how God desires to see men and women come to a saving knowledge of Him. And, she talked about the responsibility and honor of praying that someone would come to know Jesus as their Savior and Lord.

She told her to pray, as the 2 Timothy passage you read says, exercising patience with the unbeliever in hopes that God would grant salvation.

About the time Mom realized the ice cream was melting and we needed to get home to put it in the refrigerator, the lady asked Mom to teach her how to pray for her husband's salvation.

Mom talked about the lady praying for her husband all through the day as things about him come to mind. She told the lady to talk with God in the same way she had been talking to us.

"Ask God to save your husband," she told her. "Ask God to have mercy on your husband. Ask Him to soften your husband's heart."

When we got home, Mom asked me if I would put the groceries up while she continued talking with the lady. Next thing I knew, they were on their knees on the driveway praying.

This lady learned to pray for her husband's salvation and for the salvation of many others whom she knew. We prayed for this lady's husband to come to know Jesus for the next three decades.

One night, just as we were about to sit down for supper, Mom answered the telephone. All of a sudden, Mom started shouting, "Hallelujah! Thank You, Lord!" And then, as she often did, she began to sing, "To God Be the Glory." This lady's husband had come to Christ!

Prayer: Heavenly Father, thank You for the honor of praying for our unbelieving family and friends. Help us love unbelievers and treat them with gentleness. In Your name, we pray. Amen.

Ponder this: This lady prayed for thirty years that her husband would be saved. She never gave up praying. Are there those in your family or among your friends for whose salvation you need to be praying? Pray the Lord would "open their hearts so that they believe the gospel" (Acts 16:14).

Whatever It Takes
Read: Hebrews 12:7-11

For the moment, all discipline seems painful rather than pleasant, but later, it yields the peaceful fruit of righteousness to those who have been trained by it.
Hebrews 12:11

A dear friend, whom I'll call Em, allowed the circumstances of life to overwhelm her as deep roots of anger grew into bitterness toward God. The details of those circumstances are not important, but what is important is that she chose not to trust God. In fact, she set out to prove she didn't need God at all!

Soon Em quit calling her parents and everyone else. She didn't want to have anything to do with us because she knew we would talk to her about honoring God, and that was the last thing she wanted to hear.

I began praying for Em and asked my pastor to join me in praying for her, too. My pastor caught me a little off-guard when he asked, "Are you ready to pray that God will do whatever is necessary to get her attention?"

Well, no! I wasn't! After all, I didn't want Em to endure any more hardships. And then, through God's Word, I was reminded that the prayer she most needed me to pray was "Lord, do whatever it takes to bring Em back to yourself!"

"But…"

Could I really trust God enough to ask Him to do whatever

was necessary? I knew Em very well, and she was just about as stubborn as me, so I knew the "whatever" would have to be severe. What would God have to do to get her attention?

I went home, grabbed my Bible, began reading and praying, asking God to help me trust Him. I finally fell asleep after midnight, and around 3:00 a.m. I sat straight up in bed wide awake. I listened to hear what woke me up, but all was silent. I lay back down and began thinking about Em, and I prayed, "Lord, do whatever it takes to bring Em back to you." And, then I fell fast asleep.

The obnoxious ring of the telephone woke me up at 6:30 a.m. It was Em's dad. Em had been mugged, beaten, and left in a dark alley bleeding profusely.

"She may not live."

A police officer on regular patrol discovered her and found her dad's business card stuck in Em's wallet with her driver's license.

Em lived, and as the Lord used that long recovery time to heal her physically, He was also healing her spiritually and emotionally.

About a year later, Em and I were at her parents' having supper, and Em began talking about how grateful she was that the mugging occurred, because had it not happened she didn't think she would have been alive to be sitting at her parents' table for supper.

Enormous tears began flowing down her dad's face, as he began speaking slowly, "Before we went to bed that night, Mom and I prayed that the Lord would do whatever He needed to do to bring you back to Him."

He went on to explain the long process of them coming to

the point of being able to pray that prayer. I also shared with them my experience of not wanting to pray that same prayer.

In the years since this happened, I have studied the Bible and sought to know God more so that I would trust Him more. I have come to understand that it is through those "whatever it takes" moments that the Lord chips away the sharp, sinful edges in our lives as we become more and more sanctified (made into the image of Christ).

Now, instead of being afraid to pray that God would do whatever it takes in my life or the life of a loved one, I can pray with confidence that God will work in and through a person's life and circumstances in such a way that they are confronted with their weaknesses and recognize their only hope is in a vibrant, consistent relationship with Jesus Christ. In today's focal passage, we understand that while we are experiencing God's disciplining grace, which is indeed painful, that discipline produces the fruit of righteousness. That means we will know Him at a deeper level that enables us to trust Him more.

Instead of being afraid to pray, "Lord, whatever it takes," let's pray it more consistently for ourselves and others so that we are made more into the image of Christ as we learn to trust and love Him more and are strengthened to obey Him more.

Prayer: Heavenly Father, forgive us for not trusting You. Teach us who You are so that we will know that You are trustworthy. Lord, do whatever is necessary in our lives to make us more like You. In the name of Jesus, I pray. Amen.

Ponder: Do you know God well enough to pray, "Lord, do whatever it takes" for yourself or a loved one? What things come to mind that hinder you from praying like this?

For Godly Wisdom and Sanctified Common Sense

Read: James 1:1-8

If any of you lacks wisdom, you should ask God, who gives generously to all without finding fault, and it will be given him.
James 1:5 (NIV)

While living in Northern Virginia, I was faced with a big decision, and I knew that regardless of my choice, I would live with it for the rest of my life. We can say that about any choice that we face, but this was one of those life-altering decisions.

I talked with my parents about it, and they suggested things I needed to consider with each choice. They prayed with me over the phone and just before we hung up, I said, "Daddy, I don't know what the best thing would be! How do I decide?"

My dad's response was quick, "Sweetheart, use godly wisdom and sanctified common sense!"

Thinking about this situation and my dad's comment, I drove toward home in bright sunshine but with dark clouds on the horizon. I recalled James chapter 1. As a mature Christ-follower, James understood that when things around us are calm and clear, it is fairly easy to walk as a Christ-follower, just as driving home in sunshine was relaxing and easy. Add the big decisions and storms of life that may hit us, and we are easily driven off the path we as Christ-followers are to travel.

There is a series of children's books, *The Jungle Doctor*

Fables, written in the 1950s by Australian Paul White, who was a missionary to Tanganyika (now Tanzania). Narrated by Bwana, the Chief Doctor, African jungle animals are the main characters of his fables that always have a biblical truth lesson in them.

In this series, when the young monkeys who have not learned how to make their way in the jungles do something unwise, the other animals refer to it as "small monkey wisdom," which is not wisdom at all!

Unfortunately, many of us use our "small monkey wisdom" and do not even recognize our need for God's wisdom that helps us endure the trials.

When a trial hits you straight between the eyes, is your first reaction one of joy? Sadly, mine isn't! In the midst of the trials, wisdom enables us to acknowledge that God is at work in and through every situation to bring glory to Himself and to sanctify us.

In today's passage, James instructed Christians on how to not just walk through these trials that were so difficult and endure; but, to do so joyfully as he tells them to "Consider it pure joy" (v 2 NIV) when they face trials. What? How in the world am I supposed to do that?

We can react joyfully when we understand "that the testing of your faith produces endurance." And he goes on to tell them that endurance makes a Christ-follower mature and complete, lacking nothing. He continues, "If any of you lacks wisdom, you should ask God, who gives generously to all…" James makes the point that Christ-followers must be submitted to this sanctifying process when he says, "let endurance have its perfect result."

One other important thing James tells us we need in order to joyfully endure trials is wisdom from God.

I remember a sermon I heard on this passage, when the pastor explained that when James says, "If any of you lack wisdom," he isn't saying some Christ-followers have the wisdom needed to face trials and others don't, he's implying that we do not always recognize our need for God's wisdom.

This is an important point—to recognize our need for God's wisdom. Too often, we try to figure things out on our own. Wisdom is more than knowing and obeying God's Word. Wisdom also involves sound discernment as to how we apply God's Word in the circumstances and trials, which God's Word does not address specifically. It appears this is what Paul had in mind when he wrote, "but be transformed by the renewing of your mind, that you may prove what is that good and acceptable and perfect will of God" (Romans 12:2). In Colossians 1:9, Paul says "to ask that you may be filled with the knowledge of His will in all wisdom and spiritual understanding."

So, whether God's Word tells us how it should be applied to a specific circumstance or not, we gain God's wisdom by continually renewing our minds by and through His Word. That results in our having sanctified common sense.

Prayer: Father, we know that we need Your wisdom. We pray that You will give us godly wisdom and sanctified common sense so that the decisions we make throughout each day glorify You! In the name of Jesus, we pray. Amen.

Ponder this: We often struggle using our "small monkey wisdom" to figure out what we need to do in the situations we face. God invites us to come to Him praying for wisdom, and He promises to generously give us wisdom.

For Harvest Laborers
Read: Matthew 9:35-38

Therefore, pray earnestly to the Lord of the harvest
to send out laborers into his harvest.
Matthew 9:38 (NIV)

This passage has been the foundation of many teachings, sermons, and Bible readings, so it is one with which I am very familiar. And, sadly, sometimes my familiarity with a Scripture passage tempts me to fast-forward to the next passage.

In addition to this being contrary to what the Bible teaches us—to study, memorize, meditate, contemplate, and be renewed through Scripture—fast-forwarding puts us in a position of not learning what the Holy Spirit has for us to learn about God, ourselves, what we should do, and quite often, our sin.

Skipping over this particular passage with "I already know this," is not only arrogant on our part, as we think the Holy Spirit can't teach us anything more about the passage; it also robs us of the opportunity to know God better, understand ourselves and our sin better, and to be challenged to be a part of not only praying but going and financially supporting those who go.

Let's see what this passage tells us.

While Jesus was doing the things His Father sent Him to earth to do: teach, preach, and heal, "He was moved with compassion for them, because they were weary" (NKJV). Jesus saw right into the hearts of the people, and regardless of their pretense He saw their misery and pain, as people who were lost and absolutely without hope.

Next, Jesus tells His disciples, "The harvest is truly plentiful." Jesus saw in all of these people the potential of lives being transformed by the grace, mercy, and power of the gospel!

As Jesus continues telling them "the laborers are few," He is pointing out that in order to meet the great need of sharing the gospel with so many, more are needed who are willing to go and share the gospel.

Don't miss this next point. As soon as Jesus explained the severity of the situation, He immediately said, "Pray." What a wonderful example and lesson for us to learn today. When we are made aware of a situation our first thought or action should be to pray. This reminds us that yes, we are to share the gospel, and that it is only God who can change a heart.

As we pray that the Lord would bring forth workers to share the gospel, our burden for the lost will increase. As our burden increases, our prayers increase; and, the Lord often uses these prayers to give us a desire to be a part of going and telling. For all, it means sharing the gospel with those whom the Lord puts in your path. For some, it means full-time ministry in the United States or overseas. For others, it means financial support that enables others to go.

Turn on or read the news at any given moment in time, and you will get just a snippet of the myriad of ways that the harvest is plentiful in our world today. Pray asking the Lord how He would have you participate in sharing the gospel as His Holy Spirit reaps the harvest.

Prayer: Heavenly Father, forgive me for not seeing people and their needs through Your eyes, and give me eyes to see the spiritual need of those around me. Give me boldness to share the gospel with all those with whom I come in contact. In Jesus' name, I pray. Amen.

Ponder this: Take a few minutes to jot down the spiritual needs of your family (immediate and extended), your church family, your co-workers, your neighbors. Now, jot down the spiritual needs of your governmental leaders, your community, your city, your state, your nation, and the world. Pray, asking the Lord to give you wisdom and discernment in how to reach all of these with the gospel, the only true hope and help for meeting their spiritual needs.

For Their Faith Not to Fail

Read: 1 Peter 1:3-5

"But I have prayed for you that your faith may not fail.
And you, when you have turned back,
strengthen your brothers."
Luke 22:32

I was probably nine or ten years old when the following occurred, but I still remember the truths my mom and dad taught me that evening.

At supper, Mom and Dad were talking about some friends of ours who were in ministry. Dad was relaying to Mom all the things that were happening in this family's life. We already knew about their teenage son drowning while swimming in the ocean. Now the wife's mom had had a massive stroke and had come to their home for care. The leader of the organization with which this couple ministered had been fired because of sin. And now, the wife was expecting (in those days you didn't say "pregnant" in polite company), but she was experiencing some problems and they were not sure if the baby would live.

Through tears, Mom and Dad prayed. They prayed about the things I would normally hear them praying: Lord, give them strength. Lord, give the doctors wisdom to know how to care for this woman and her unborn child. And then, my dad prayed something similar to this, "Lord, I pray their faith would not fail as they look to You for the strength and courage they need to walk trusting You."

I suppose I had my perplexed "I don't really know what that means" look on my face because my mom asked me if something was wrong.

I explained that I didn't know your faith could fail—especially not the faith of that couple whom I knew served God.

Dad explained that it is impossible for saving faith to fail. We are given supernatural faith by grace and mercy from God that enables us to believe in the gospel and in Jesus Christ, which brings us to a saving or true knowledge of God. A true Christ-follower will not lose His faith in Christ, nor will He reject Christ as Lord nor the gospel. Today's passage speaks to this.

He further explained that Christ-followers might fall into grievous sin as a result of the choices made when tempted by the evil one or our own sinful desires, or through the sinful influence of those around us, often because we have not been diligent to be in the Word, to pray, to sit under the teaching and preaching of the Word, and to fellowship with other believers.

When you pray that someone's faith will not fail, you are praying that her faith would remain strong and her resolve to honor God in and through everything would remain strong so that she would not make sinful choices.

Today's focal passage context is Jesus telling Peter he will deny Him. Jesus models for us the importance of praying when we know someone is in the midst of great turmoil, suffering, and temptation to which they may succumb in sin.

As we become aware of the things going on in the lives of those around us, we can pray that their faith will not fail. And we know that even if they succumb to temptation and sin, they can repent and be restored to their relationship with their Savior and

Lord.

The last part of this verse offers hope, for if you are a true Christ-follower, even if you sin you can repent and return to Christ. Jesus says, once you repent and return, "strengthen your brethren." Encourage them with your testimony of God's grace, and uphold them through your prayers.

Prayer: Father God, I pray that our faith will not fail. That we would be diligent to be in the Word and walk closely with You. I pray that as You strengthen us, we would be compelled to pray that the faith of others would not fail. In the name of Jesus, I pray. Amen.

Ponder this: By God's grace, and our obedience to His Word, our faith will not fail. We can stand firm against the temptation to sin by the grace and mercy of God. Who do you know that is in the midst of a great deal of turmoil, suffering, and temptation? Begin right now to pray that her faith will not fail. Make an effort to encourage her through a text, email, note, phone call, or visit.

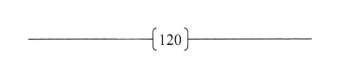

Chapter Six
Meditations about Prayer from the Old Testament

Harriet

In Times Like These
Read: Genesis 18:23-28

Now Abraham arose early in the morning and went to the place where he had stood before the Lord; and looked down toward Sodom and Gomorrah, and toward all the land of the valley, and he saw, and behold the smoke of the land ascended like the smoke of a furnace.
Genesis 19:27-28 (NASB)

There is a hymn entitled "In Times Like These," written in the 1950s by Ruth Caye Jones, that talks about how desperately we need God to anchor us during difficult times.

Have you ever been through those kinds of times— agonizingly difficult ones? I have. I have had situations in my life that were extremely challenging, even gut-wrenching, and much too personal to write about. But I remember them well.

Can you remember things you've agonized over? Maybe you are experiencing such a time right now. Abraham had a time like this in today's passage.

In the previous passage of Genesis 18:23-32, God told Abraham He was going to destroy the cities of Sodom and Gomorrah because of their wickedness. Abraham's nephew Lot lived in this area, and Abraham loved Lot very much. So, Abraham pleaded with God to spare the righteous people who lived in the city, which he knew would include his beloved nephew.

God listened to Abraham's request and agreed to save the cities even if only ten righteous people could be found living in them. But sadly, there were not even ten. Still, Genesis 19:29 tells us "so it was that when God destroyed the cities of the valley, God remembered Abraham and sent Lot out of the midst." God did not spare the city, but because of Abraham's petitions, He spared Lot. God answered Abraham's prayer and did not let the righteous perish with the wicked.

But Abraham didn't know that on the morning the smoke of Sodom and Gomorrah rose up from the valley below him. The Scripture tells us that on the morning the cities were destroyed, Abraham went back to the place where he had stood before the Lord. He looked down toward Sodom and Gomorrah and saw the smoke from the burning cities.

What a poignant scene. I can just see Abraham getting up early after a sleepless night and scurrying to a vantage point to see if the cities had been destroyed. It must have taken his breath away to see the cities burning. He would have known there had not even been ten righteous people in the city. And he would have assumed his nephew had perished along with the rest of the city.

Another old hymn, "He Hideth My Soul" by Fanny J. Crosby, comes to my mind in times like these. Its refrain says:

> He hideth my soul in the cleft of the rock,
> That shadows a dry, thirsty land;
> He hideth my life in the depths of His love,
> And covers me there with His hand,
> And covers me there with His hand.

I've lived in a hot, thirsty land. During the dry season in Nigeria, the land becomes dry, dusty, barren, and yes, one gets very hot and thirsty. There is a section of this country that has huge rock formations as big as small mountains. I have climbed these rocks as a child and can remember the comfort of finding a cleft that blocked the sun where I could sit and rest a while.

Abraham's prayer was answered, though he did not know it at the time he was agonizing over the burning city. How many times are our prayers already answered too, but we fret and worry anyway because we cannot see the answer for ourselves?

Prayer: Heavenly Father, be near to us in difficult times. Speak to us in Your still, small voice, comforting us. Gently draw us closer to You. Thank You for hearing and answering our heartfelt prayers, in Jesus' name. Amen.

Ponder this: God's anchor holds. Like the cleft of a rock, He shelters you, even in the most difficult times. Are you in need of his shelter right now?

Poured Out Like Water
Read: 1 Samuel 1:10-15

Arise, cry out in the night, as the watches of the night begin;
pour out your heart like water in the presence of the Lord...
Lamentations 2:19a (NIV)

Back in our school days, we were probably all taught about the viscosity of liquids. The word viscosity refers to how thick a liquid is; some are thick and gooey while other liquids are thin and flow easily. If for example, you take corn syrup and water and pour them out onto a surface, you will see the difference. Corn syrup is more viscous and pours out slowly, sort of clumping as it hits the surface. Water, on the other hand, pours quickly and freely, soon spilling out over the edge of the counter onto the floor. The corn syrup will eventually progress to the end of the counter too but more slowly, giving you more time to grab a paper towel and clean it up before it hits the floor.

Interestingly, God tells us to pour our hearts out to Him like water, not corn syrup. This implies freely telling God everything that burdens us, holding nothing back. Hannah did this when she prayed for a child. She prayed so earnestly and fervently that Eli the priest thought she was drunk. He could see her lips moving but could not hear any sound coming from her because she was speaking so softly. Eli scolded her for drinking so early in the day, but she explained that she was not drunk at all; she was pouring her heart out to God. Hannah desperately wanted a child so she turned to God knowing that only He could grant this petition and give her the desire of her heart.

God is pleased when we pour out our hearts to Him. There are other places in Scripture where we are told to pour our hearts out to God. Psalm 62:8 (NIV) says, "Trust in him at all times, you people; pour out your heart to him, for God is our refuge." And Isaiah 26:16 says, "O Lord, in distress they sought you; they poured out a whispered prayer when your discipline was upon them."

Isn't that a beautiful passage—pouring out a whispered prayer? Have you ever poured out a whispered prayer like Hannah? Have you ever felt like the prayer on your heart was so deep and personal, you could only whisper it to God? When those times come, picture the prayer being poured out freely like water from a glass. Do not be afraid to come freely to God with even these—your deepest, most secret desires.

I had a prayer like this once. My husband and I had three children, the oldest of which was about to start high school. Unknown to anyone, I began to desire another child. I didn't dare share this with anyone, including my husband. It was all I could do to whisper it to God. But I did tell God about it. Sheepishly, I confessed my desire to Him, as though it were a feeling I should not have. I asked God to take the desire away from me because I fully believed it impossible to ever have another child. For many long months, I asked God to take the desire away and waited expectantly for that to happen.

But God had other plans. To my delight and my husband's surprise, God chose to give us another child. So, when our other children were ages 15, 12, and 11, when I was 39 and my husband was 41... our fourth and last child was born. We once again were the proud parents of a bouncing baby boy who has either kept us young or made us old before our time—we're not sure which.

God answered Hannah's prayer too. He gave her a son whom she named Samuel. In 1 Samuel 1:27 we read Hannah's famous words, "For this child, I have prayed, and the Lord has granted me my petition." Then in chapter 2, after Samuel was born, Hannah prayed a beautiful prayer of thanksgiving and praise.

Prayer: Gracious Heavenly Father, thank You for Your great love toward us. Thank You for letting us tell You anything and everything that is on our hearts. Thank You for answered prayers, and for lessons learned when they are not answered the way we had hoped. Thank You for letting us pour our hearts out to You, in Jesus' name. Amen.

Ponder this: You can tell God anything. What have you been holding back and need to confess or ask Him about?

Constant Prayer

Read: 1 Samuel 7:8, 12:23, 7:13

As for me, far be it from me that I should sin against the LORD
by failing to pray for you.
And I will teach you the way that is good and right.
1 Samuel 12:23 (NIV)

"Please, please, please, Mommy!"

"Honey, don't bother me about that again. I've heard your request, and I know you want me to say yes. But I haven't made a decision yet, so stop asking me!"

"But please!"

"I said, don't ask again!"

I have had conversations like this with my children many times; and when I was a child, I had these same conversations with my mother. My mom tells me of all her four children, I was the worst at begging. I used to pester her terribly if I wanted something. She would proclaim the "mother's curse," as she jokingly called it, telling me she hoped I grew up to have children just like me—ones that would pester me as much as I pestered her.

A parent's reaction to this badgering is human nature. We get irritated at the constant requests and frustrated with our children for making them. Fortunately, human nature is not God's nature. God not only allows us to pester Him with our prayer requests, he actually instructs us to do exactly that.

We can see this truth played out in the life of Samuel, the Old Testament priest. In the fourth chapter of 1 Samuel, the sons of Eli, Samuel's mentor, were killed by the Philistines in an attack that caused Israel to flee and many to be slaughtered. When Eli heard the news, he fell backward in shock and broke his neck, causing his death as well. The people were very frightened and asked Samuel to pray for them. The Israelites were a humble group at this point in time. 1 Samuel 7:6 says that they gathered at Mizpah, fasted, and said, "We have sinned against the Lord." Then, a couple of verses later, they go one step further. More than just asking Samuel to pray for them, they ask him never to stop praying for them. In other words, they asked Samuel to pray for them continually, without ceasing.

How did Samuel respond? Did he respond like an irritated parent? Did he remind the people that he had already prayed for them? Did he ask them to stop pestering him? No, in contrast to the way I and other exasperated parents often answer their children, Samuel willingly agreed to the people's request. We see this in today's key verse when he says, "As for me, far be it from me that I should sin against the LORD by failing to pray for you."

Did Samuel's practice of praying for the people help? 1 Samuel 7:13 tells us that it did indeed. This passage says the "hand of the Lord was against the Philistines all the days of Samuel." There is no doubt a connection between the fact that Samuel did not stop lifting the people up to God in prayer and God's hand continuing to be against their enemy all of Samuel's life.

This truth can be found other places in Scripture, too. 1 Thessalonians 5:17 instructs us to pray without ceasing. In Luke 18:1-8 we find the story of the persistent widow who kept pestering a judge for a favorable ruling in her case. Jesus told this parable for the express purpose of showing that we should pray persistently and not lose heart. And in Isaiah 62:6-7 (NIV) we read these words: "I have posted watchmen on your walls, Jerusalem; they will never be silent day or night. You who call on the LORD, give yourselves no rest, and give him no rest till he establishes Jerusalem and makes her the praise of the earth."

Prayer: Heavenly Father, You are our Abba, our Daddy. Your Spirit is patient, and You love it when Your children talk to You. Thank You for showing us in Your Word that we can and should come to You over and over. Teach us to not lose heart but to grow in our own patience as we wait expectantly for Your answers to our prayers, in Jesus' name. Amen.

Ponder this: It's okay to pester God. He wants us to pray without ceasing. So, go ahead! Pester Him all you want about all that concerns you.

Walking Humbly
Read: Daniel 9:3-7

He has shown you, O mortal, what is good. And what does the
Lord require of you? To act justly and to love mercy
and to walk humbly with your God.
Micah 6:8 (NIV)

When I was about two years old, the well-known evangelist, Billy Graham, visited Nigeria, West Africa, where my parents served as missionaries. One of his stops was our little town of Ogbomoso. The missionaries planned a large reception in his honor. The women worked for weeks preparing for the arrival of this great man. My older sister, Alisa, was all of four years old at the time.

When the day finally arrived and the honored guest was among us, to my mother's horror, little four-year-old Alisa made her way, unattended, to the food table. There her eyes fell on all the delicious, beautifully displayed items that had been so lovingly made by the missionary wives. Her eyes especially noticed the large cake with its rich white icing. Though we had ingredients for sweets in this tropical land where sugar cane grew, we didn't have an abundance of goods, so something like a cake was a rare treat. When my mother saw Alisa eyeing the cake, Mom made a beeline her way.

But before my mother could get to her, Alisa lifted her hand and ran her index finger all around the bottom of the plate at the edge of the cake until she had a large glob of icing on it. This she proceeded to quickly pop into her mouth, making smacking sounds as she licked her finger clean. My mom hurriedly made her way to her four-year-old daughter and was just about to discipline Alisa for her poor manners when the great man himself stepped in between them. Smiling at the antics of a four-year-old, Reverend Graham raised his hand in a "stop" gesture and told my mother, "Oh, leave her alone. She's just a child."

My mother was embarrassed because, aside from it being poor manners to lick one's fingers or run them around cake icing, my sister was a small, unimportant child compared to the greatness of the man for whom the cake had been made. But Reverend Graham showed his humility when he graciously asked for mercy on Alisa's behalf. Yet, the difference in greatness between a four-year-old child and a world-famous evangelist pales in comparison to the difference between mankind, the creation, and God, the Creator.

Humility is a common thread among prayer warriors in the Bible. The apostle Paul called himself the chief of sinners in 1 Timothy 1:15. Nehemiah wept and mourned for days before he came to the Lord in prayer over the deteriorated condition of the Jerusalem wall. And, Daniel said in his prayers that the people deserved open shame for the sins they had committed.

Daniel made a very descriptive contrast between man and God in today's passage when he wrote that the people had sinned, acted wickedly, rebelled, turned away from God's ordinances, and had not listened to God. And by comparison, what does Daniel say about God? These beautiful words can be found in chapter 2, verses 20–22. In the NIV it reads:

"Praise be to the name of God forever and ever;

wisdom and power are his.
He changes times and seasons;
He deposes kings and raises up others.
He gives wisdom to the wise and
knowledge to the discerning.
He reveals deep and hidden things;
He knows what lies in darkness,
and light dwells with him."

And yet, this great and awesome God, as Daniel calls Him, came down to earth to live as a man. And He died to offer us mercy. This mighty God, who can change the times and seasons and reveals deep and hidden things, came to earth as a little baby and lived among His creation. He died a brutal death on the cross so our sins could be forgiven and we could gain eternal life.

Reverend Graham asked for mercy for my older sister when she was about to receive punishment. Jesus Christ did more than that. He took the punishment for us on the cross.

Prayer: Heavenly Father, the great and awesome God that You are, thank You for stooping down and offering us Your mercy. Help us to see Your greatness as You also make us aware of our unworthiness. Teach us to walk humbly with You, in Jesus' name. Amen.

Ponder this: Great is the Lord, and He is worthy of our praise. Do you long for humility? Recognizing God's greatness naturally humbles us. Get your mind off yourself and focus on God's greatness today.

All Prayed Up!
Read: Ezra 5:11-6:1

*This is the answer they gave us: "We are the servants of the
God of heaven and earth…"*
Ezra 5:11a (NIV)

"Explain yourself, young lady!"

How many times did I hear my mother use this phrase when
I was a child? Far too many, as I recall. Whenever she said it, she
was usually standing in front of me with a scowl on her face and
a hand on her hip. Sometimes disapproval showed on her face,
but other times she looked confused and concerned. Of course,
when I became a parent, I used the phrase with my children, too.
It was our way of gaining understanding of the child's actions,
choices, or situation.

In today's passage, that is exactly what the children of Israel
did—they explained themselves and their actions to King Darius.
The Jews saw an opportunity to rebuild the temple and took it.
But their actions raised questions in the minds of those around
them, especially Tattenai, the governor, and his assistant. So, the
Jews carefully explained themselves in a letter to the king,
knowing full well that the governor would have to abide by
whatever King Darius decided and decreed.

They had the law on their side, and they knew it. In verse 13,
their letter cited a royal decree that had been made many years
earlier but had never been fulfilled. They were so certain of their

legal position, they even suggested the king make a search of the royal archives to verify this unfulfilled decree that they claimed existed. But more importantly, they had God on their side. Verse 5 tells us that the eye of the Lord was watching over them.

This is a good lesson for us. We should always be ready to give an answer or explanation about our prayer concerns— whether to God in our prayers or to others after we have spent time praying about whatever the situation might be.

My mother was a country girl, born and raised on a farm in rural North Carolina. She sometimes used the expression, "all prayed up." It meant that she had spent much time in prayer and was ready to act on her prayers. In today's passage, the Israelite people were all prayed up, to use my mother's term. They took action and were ready with an explanation for their action.

In Ezra 6:1, King Darius not only agreed with the action the Israelites took—rebuilding the temple—but he also issued a decree to search for and return the lost temple treasures. Imagine their immense joy when they once again worshiped in their beloved temple, filled again with its treasures. It all sounds so great and it was wonderful. This story has a happy ending.

But does that mean God's stories always have happy endings? Well, the long-term answer to that question is a resounding yes, but sometimes the short-term answer is a frustrating no. In Ecclesiastes 9:1 (NIV), wise Solomon offers this sobering reminder, "...the righteous and the wise and what they do are in God's hands, but no one knows whether love or hate awaits them."

I would add that no man knows whether success or failure await him either. But whether success or failure, whether ease or difficulty, certain truths remain: get "prayed up" by spending much time in prayer over your life and the things God has laid on your heart to do, then do them eagerly, and be ready to give an answer to others and to God.

Prayer: Heavenly Father, You alone hold all things in Your hands. Use us in Your work as You would want, and help us to trust You when we feel discouraged. Amen.

Ponder this: What is God calling you to do? Are you trusting Him with the success or failure of it?

Chapter Seven

Musical Prayers

Day 1
Piano Prayers
Read: **Ephesians 5:17-20**

*Let the word of Christ dwell in you richly in all wisdom, teaching
and admonishing one another in psalms and hymns and
spiritual songs, singing with grace in your hearts to the Lord.*
Colossians 3:16 (NKJV)

Those who know me understand how much I love music,
particularly piano music, as an expression of worship. My dad
taught me to use music as an expression of worship by teaching
me that music is much more than correctly played notes. He
taught me that as I play the piano, the notes, combined with the
dynamics, express my awe, love, and gratitude to the Sovereign
God of the universe. Music is one of my ways of pouring out my
heart—praying—to God. Through the music, I confess my sin,
admit my dependence upon Him, ask Him for strength, thank
Him for His gift of salvation, and praise Him for who He is.

I like to create hymn medley arrangements for the offertories
I play. I learned some time ago to always add the lyrics to the
scores in order to remain aware of the meaning of the music I am
playing, so that through those words I can express my worship to
the Lord.

Music is a wonderful gift from God. As we walk through the
woods or the jungle, we hear the beautiful singing of birds, the
lilting chatter of monkeys, the deep croaking of frogs, the hissing
of a snake, the loud claps of thunder, the majestic trumpeting of

an elephant, the sound of the rushing wind, or a trickling mountain stream—all of these are beautiful music.

Music calms, comforts, encourages, stirs our souls and emotions to action, and can help strengthen our resolve as the Holy Spirit applies the music to our hearts.

Sadly, today, many people equate worship with music. Music is not worship, it is one of the ways we express our worship. Some lack an understanding that all of life is worship, and the worship service includes various aspects of worship: prayer, reading Scripture, music (vocal and instrumental), preaching and teaching Scripture, and giving of our tithes and offerings.

From the passage you read today, we understand that our singing is the result of being filled with or controlled by the Holy Spirit, which is contrasted with being drunk with wine. When the Holy Spirit fills us, our lives overflow with God's Word. Our singing is to be honest and heartfelt. And we are to sing to the Lord, so our music is to be God-focused, not self-focused.

The next verse tells us that our singing is to have a sound biblical understanding of who God is so that we can indeed give Him thanks for everything because we trust Him.

Our Ephesians 5 reading and today's focal passage both tell us to sing to each other, which means to sing together in corporate worship as we testify about God, encourage each other in the Lord, and place our corporate focus on God.

We then read that we are to use various kinds of music to glorify God, teach sound doctrine, and encourage each other.

Prayer: Father, thank You for the gift of music through which we express our awe, love, and gratitude to You; pour out our hearts to You; confess our sin, admit our dependence upon You, ask You for strength, thank You for Your gift of salvation, and praise You for who You are, in the name of Jesus. Amen.

Ponder this: Contemplate the expressions of worship found in some of your favorite music. How do these songs stir your heart? What songs do you sing when you are heavy laden? Learn several biblical songs—both old and new—that help you express your worship of God.

Take Time to Be Holy
Read: 1 Peter 1:13-21

Pursue peace with all men, and holiness without which
no one will see the Lord.
Hebrews 12:14 (NKJV)

My dad taught me much about music as an expression of my worship and communication with God, and my mom modeled for me how to use music to praise God, to give Him thanks for His provision and blessings, to express absolute dependence upon Him, to pour out my cares and concerns, and much more.

I treasure the memories of many wonderful road trips with my mom. We would visit family and friends, go to funerals, and just go places we wanted to visit. We would talk, and laugh, and sing. If we set out in the early morning, she would begin singing a wonderful hymn of praise—at least it was for her—"Oh, What a Beautiful Morning" (from *Oklahoma!*). Without a break, she might sing, "This is My Father's World," and then go into "How Great Thou Art," or "He's Got the Whole World in His Hands." If we passed a pasture with cattle she would sing, "My Father Owns the Cattle on a Thousand Hills." She would then quote a Scripture passage the scene brought to her mind and talk about the greatness of God.

One of the hymns that I often heard her sing was "Take Time to Be Holy." William D. Longstaff wrote the beautiful words, and George C. Stebbins wrote the melody. When things would get a little hectic, and she wasn't sure how to get everything done, I would hear her singing this hymn. Once a friend who was quite upset came to visit mom. I was sitting at the dining room table doing homework. They sat at the kitchen table drinking iced tea as the woman began crying and told Mom of all her burdens, hurts, and fears. I wasn't really paying attention to their conversation until there was a prolonged period of silence.

Then I heard my mom sing:

Take time to be holy, speak oft with Thy Lord;

Abide in Him always and feed on His word...

She then began to explain to this woman the importance of being holy as you read in today's passage in 1 Peter. She spoke of the importance of knowing God through His Word, and of communicating—or praying—to God. Mom explained to the woman that prayer is a constant communication with God. She continued using each phrase of the hymn to explain who God is and how we are to communicate with Him and be obedient to His Word.

The bottom line, which we see in the 1 Peter passage and today's focal passage, is that our holiness doesn't just happen in a vacuum. She continued by teaching the woman about God and holiness:

- Jesus is the only hope anyone has in times of trouble.
- The more you know God, the more you will trust Him. You will not trust whom you do not know.
- We are to use the Word of God as the standard by which we measure our heart motivations, not our own standards, nor those of someone else.
- When the Spirit of God convicts you of sin, repent and make it right vertically with God and horizontally with

your brothers and sisters.

♦ You cannot "be holy as I am holy" (1 Peter 3:15) with unconfessed sin abiding in and ruling your heart.

Mom's prayer life modeled how to pray as she began communicating with God from the moment she woke up in the morning until she closed her eyes to sleep at night. She thanked Him for clean running water, for electricity, for a parking space close to the grocery store entrance, and so on. Whenever she had a decision to make, she would pray, "God, help me know what You would like me to do." When she was heading out to minister to someone who was hurting she would pray, "Lord, give me strength and the right words to say!"

Prayer: Father we thank You for showing us how to pray, and for praying for us! Thank You that You do not expect us to be holy without the work of Your Holy Spirit in our lives, in Jesus' name. Amen.

Ponder this: Prayer is an integral part of being holy. How is the consistency and fervency of your prayer life contributing to your holiness?

My Faith Looks Up to Thee
Read: Hebrews 6:13-20

Looking unto Jesus, the author and finisher of our faith,
who for the joy that was set before Him endured the cross,
despising the shame, and has sat down
at the right hand of the throne of God.
Hebrews 12:1-2 (NKJV)

One morning, I stood at the window drinking a cup of coffee and watching a couple of doves fly onto and perch upon an air handling system that was surrounded by an 8-foot-high fence. They sat on the unit, walked around it, and flew from one side of it to the next as they explored. They flew to the ground and busied themselves with finding seeds, grass, weeds, and other things to eat.

After a few minutes, they were ready to go and began trying to figure a way out of the fenced-in area. They flew straight across and barely missed hitting the fence. They repeated this flight pattern in numerous directions, each time discovering no way out. Next, they flew to the ground and walked around trying to find an escape route for a long time, trying different locations in the fence—to no avail.

They seemed agitated, and to make matters worse, another bird lit just outside the fence and seemed to almost be making fun of them for not being able to get out of the fenced-in area.

Finally, one of the doves flew back to the perch on the air

handling system and began closely inspecting the fence around him, the unit below him, and then he seemed to shake in disbelief as he noticed the unbarred sky above him. Suddenly, he took off from the unit flying straight up and escaping the confinement of the fenced-in area.

This dove flew around for a little while and then perched on the top edge of the fence and began flapping his wings as if trying to get the other dove's attention. Although I couldn't hear anything because I was inside the building (and, incidentally, I don't speak dove), I imagine this dove's wing flapping was accompanied by his chirping to the other dove, "Look up!" because in just a few seconds the other dove flew straight up and escaped.

As I thought about the interaction of the doves and other bird, I began to see a beautiful picture of God's mercy and grace in my own life.

I have often "flown" into a situation and preoccupied myself with all the stuff going on around me, only to suddenly realize I am trapped and cannot find a way out. I keep trying to find something or some way to get out of the situation, but I am really just trying the same futile things over and over while expecting a different result.

There are several biblical applications that come to mind, yet I was struck with an overwhelming sense of gratitude for the myriad of people God has brought into my life at various times. Those men and women have flapped their wings to get my attention as they called out "Look up to Jesus!" They reminded me that my only hope is in Jesus Christ, who saves and sustains me.

This scene reminded me of today's focal passage that tells us to look to Jesus, the author and finisher of our faith. Only in and through Him are we able to escape from the bondage of sin. He gives us the grace and mercy needed to continue living.

A hymn, "My Faith Looks Up to Thee," also came to mind. It is based on Ephesians 3:12, "In whom we have boldness and access with confidence through faith of Him" (NKJV). This hymn lays out how a person exercises her faith in God by looking to Him for everything—salvation, holiness, grace, strength, love, comfort, and guidance. If you are not familiar with the words, look them up in a hymnal or online. The hymn begins with a prayer asking the Lord to forgive our sin.

> My faith looks up to Thee, Thou Lamb of Calvary,
> Savior divine!
> Now hear me while I pray, Take all my guilt away,
> O let me from this day be wholly Thine!

What a beautiful prayer! It reminds us that regardless of our situation, our only hope is to look to Jesus in faith to save and sustain us. As part of a local church, we are to spur each other on to godly living by reminding each other that God is able, and to pray for one another.

Prayer: Father, thank You that when we look to You for help, You are willing and able to help us. Remind us in the midst of our struggles that our only hope is in and through our relationship with You. In the name of Jesus, I pray. Amen.

Ponder this: When you are in the midst of a struggle, do you look to Jesus for help? In what ways do you actively and intentionally encourage people to look to Jesus?

Take It to the Lord in Prayer
Read: Hebrews 4:14-16

For we do not have a high priest who is unable to
sympathize with our weaknesses,
but one who in every respect has been tempted as we are,
yet without sin.
Hebrews 4:15

At the grocery store one day, I observed an interesting situation as an elderly man was trying to use the self-checkout. He pulled his cart up to the self-checkout station and began trying to find the price bar on a loaf of bread so he could scan it. He got so frustrated, he threw the loaf of bread back in the shopping cart and picked up a can of soup. He quickly found the price bar and began waving the can back and forth over the scanner. One of the grocery store employees came up and asked if she could help the man. He just ignored her and kept trying to make the scanner work. The employee shrugged her shoulders and walked away. The man began banging the soup can on the scanner.

At about that time, a young man walked up and said, "Gramps, what are you doing?"

The elderly man retorted, "This stupid machine is broken."

The same employee walked back over and offered to help the two men, showing them how to initiate the transactions by selecting certain choices on the computer screen. Then she scanned all the items in the man's grocery cart and showed him the options to choose in order to pay for his groceries and complete the transaction.

The younger man said, "See, if you would just quit trying to figure it all out by yourself, and go to the experts, your life would work much easier."

It occurred to me that in our relationship with God, we as Christ-followers often behave just like the elderly man was behaving. Don't we? We think we can handle things in our own strength and with our own knowledge and ability, and we usually fail miserably at solving whatever situation we are trying to handle. Too often, we only think of going to the Lord in prayer after we have exhausted all our best efforts. Yet, God tells us to bring everything to him, regardless of how small or big we think it is.

One of my many favorite hymns is "What a Friend We Have in Jesus" by Joseph Scriven. Through this hymn, we are reminded to take everything to the Lord in prayer.

> Have we trials and temptations?
> Is there trouble anywhere?
> We should never be discouraged,
> Take it to the Lord in prayer.
> Can we find a friend so faithful,
> Who will all our sorrows share?
> Jesus knows our every weakness;
> Take it to the Lord in prayer.

In today's focal passage, Jesus tells us to bring all of our concerns and cares to Him because He understands them all. Other Scriptures tell us that God answers our prayers when they are prayed according to His will (1 John 5:14). We bring our fears, hurts, and hearts' desires to the Lord as we pray, trusting that He will answer our prayers according to His will.

Prayer is communication with God Almighty. In the same way that our earthly relationships dissolve without good communication, our relationship with our Heavenly Father suffers when we do not allow Him to speak to us through His Word, and we do not speak to Him in prayer.

We can bring everything to God in prayer when we know Him as our Savior. Then, we come to know God and His character better as we read, study, memorize, contemplate, and meditate upon His Word, and live in obedience to that Word.

Prayer: Gracious Father, thank You for inviting us to bring everything to You. Thank You that You consider my cares and concerns, regardless of how insignificant they may seem to me. I thank You that I can trust You with my fears and burdens. Help me to trust You enough to pray, in Jesus' name. Amen.

Ponder this: Jesus invites us to bring all our cares and concerns to Him in prayer, for He understands everything we are experiencing and He is able to answer all our requests according to His will.

Day 5
More About Jesus
Read: Philippians 3:7-11

I want to know Christ—yes, to know the power of his resurrection
and participation in his sufferings,
becoming like him in his death.
Philippians 3:10 (NIV)

A dear 100-year-old friend whom I was privileged to call "Granny" had been a Christ-follower for eighty-five years! We had wonderful conversations about the Lord, and she taught me much about the Bible, and what it means to be a Christ-follower.

It was my great honor to be at her bedside during the last thirty minutes of her life here on earth. When I entered the room, grandchildren and great-grandchildren were gathered. Granny had outlived her three children.

I made my way to her bed, spoke with and hugged each family member. As I came alongside her bed, she saw me and said, "I'm so glad you're here! Read to us from God's Word!"

So, I pulled a chair close to her bed, grabbed her Bible off the nightstand, turned to the Psalms, and began reading Psalm 1.

She said with a sweet smile on her face, "Oh, Psalms is one of my sixty-six favorite books in the Bible!"

And truly, each page of her Bible, from Genesis to Revelation was underlined and marked, with notes in the margins.

I read five Psalms I knew were very dear to her, and then

noticed a change in the monitors. About that time, the nurse came in to check her, and she whispered to a granddaughter, "It won't be long now."

With tears flowing down my face, I stood up and got close to Granny's face and said, "Granny, it won't be long until you see your Savior Jesus!"

She reached up and wiped away a tear as she said, "Oh, I can't wait to see Jesus!"

I kissed her, told her how grateful I was that the Lord had brought her into my life, told her how much I loved her, and prayed aloud, giving thanks to the Lord for the life and witness of this precious saint. Then I moved out of the way for the grandchildren and great-grandchildren to have their turn saying their farewells.

Her eyelids were getting heavy, so I asked if there was something, in particular, she wanted me to read. "Just read God's Word, I want to know"—and she began singing softly in a raspy voice—"More, more about Jesus." As I recited Psalm 23 verse 4, "Yea, though I walk through the valley of the shadow of death, I will fear no evil: for thou art with me, thy rod and thy staff they comfort me" (KJV), Granny went to meet her Savior!

I have played that scene over in my mind numerous times. Each time, I am amazed that the final request of this precious woman of God was to hear His Word read so she would know more about her Savior!

Do you know the hymn for which Eliza E. Hewitt wrote the words and John R. Sweney wrote the music? "More About Jesus" speaks to my elderly friend's last request, and today's focal passage: The first verse and chorus are:

More about Jesus would I know,

More of His grace to others show;
More of His saving fullness see,
More of His love who died for me.
More, more about Jesus,
More, more about Jesus;
More of His saving fullness see,
More of His love who died for me.

Prayer: Gracious Father, I thank You for the Holy Spirit-inspired Word that You left us so that we can know You! Thank You for those whom you place in our lives to disciple us and help us understand what it means to be a faithful follower of Christ. Give us a passion to know You more, in the name of Your Son. Amen.

Ponder this: No matter how many years you follow Christ, read, study, memorize, meditate upon, and contemplate His Word, you will never know Him on this side of Heaven well enough to stop learning about Him.

Chapter Eight
More Meditations
from the Old Testament

Harriet

When God Says No
Read: Habakkuk 3:16-19

*Though the flock should be cut off from the fold, and there be no
cattle in the stall, yet I will exult in the Lord,
I will rejoice in the Lord of my salvation.*
Habakkuk 3:17b-18 (NASB)

"There are some prayers that have not been granted, and I cannot understand why. As my human eye sees, there are a number of persons who would be very much happier and better off in every way, if the Lord could just see eye to eye with me, and answer my prayers concerning them. So far, He has not, and that is all that I know about it. But I do not plan to give up trying to learn to pray."

The above is a quote by Susan Anderson from her book, *So this is Africa*. Susan was one of the early American missionaries to Nigeria, in the first half of the twentieth century. Her book, which is now out of print, has a copyright date of 1948. At the time of her mission work, things were beginning to get a little better for missionaries to tropical lands like Nigeria, but prior to the discovery of penicillin in 1928, missionaries often packed their belongings inside a casket which they took with them because, sadly, the caskets were often needed. Many people living in tropical countries succumbed to illnesses which are now easily treated with antibiotics, antimalarials, and other drugs. Susan was a brave woman to travel alone as a single missionary to this tropical nation to share the gospel with those who had never heard. In her book, she records times when God did not seem to see eye to eye with her and answer her prayers accordingly—as she put it.

The prophet Habakkuk was in similar shoes in his day, too. In the early part of the book, Habakkuk questioned God about the injustice he saw around him. A little further on in the book, he reviewed Israel's history and God's work in that history. Habakkuk came to believe that because God worked in the past, God could be trusted with the future. It is important that he came to this conclusion because Habakkuk received a prophetic vision that caused him to fear greatly. This can be seen in chapter 3, verse 16, in the NASB, when he writes, "I heard and my inward parts trembled, at the sound, my lips quivered. Decay enters my bones and… I tremble. Because I must wait quietly for the day of distress, for the people to arise who will invade us."

Yet, Habakkuk determined in his heart that he would accept from the hand of God whatever God brought because he believed that no matter how frightened he might be or how unpleasant the fulfillment of the vision, God would be acting according to His sovereign will. And Habakkuk had already established his trust in that will. So, what did Habakkuk choose to do? He chose praise!

Evidence of Habakkuk's choice to praise God can be found in verses 17-19 (NASB) of chapter 3. In what are some of the most beautiful verses in all of Scripture, Habakkuk recounted his decision to rejoice in the Lord in spite of his circumstances and fear when he wrote, "Though the fig tree should not blossom, and there be no fruit on the vines, though the yield of the olive should fail, and the fields produce no food, though the flock should be cut off from the fold, and there be no cattle in the stalls, yet I will exalt the Lord, will rejoice in the God of my salvation. The Lord God is my strength, and He has made my feet like hind's feet, and makes me walk on my high places."

Susan, I too do not plan to give up learning more about prayer, even if, like you, I am sometimes baffled by it. This I know from Habakkuk—I can accept God's will no matter how it affects me. And regardless of my circumstances, I can choose to praise Him.

Prayer: Heavenly Father, You are good. You can be trusted with our futures, even if they seem scary and difficult. Please hold our hands through the tough times, keep our hearts steadfast on You, and comfort us with Your Spirit, in your Son's name. Amen.

Ponder this: What prayers have you prayed that you feel God said no to? Is there something heavy on your heart right now? God can be trusted with all of our concerns.

Be Amazed!
Read: Habakkuk 1:1-5, Jeremiah 37:17-19

Look among the nations! Observe! Be astonished! Wonder!
Because I am doing something in your days—
you would not believe if you were told.
Habakkuk 1:5 (NASB)

Look, wonder, be amazed!

What encouraging words! They almost sound magical to me. If I heard someone speak these words to me, I would expect to see something on a grand scale, the likes of which I had never seen before. What would you expect to see if you heard words like this directed at you? A new car? News that you had just won a trip or a large sum of money?

In Habakkuk 1:5, God spoke these words to Habakkuk in response to his prayer. In verses 1-4, Habakkuk complained to God about the injustice around him. Verse 1 makes it clear that he had been crying out to God about this for some time. In that verse, he said (NASB), "How long, O Lord, will I call for help, and you will not hear?"

Have you ever cried out to God and prayed earnestly about something but you didn't think God was listening? Surely, Habakkuk felt that God was not listening, nor answering the prayer he had been praying for so long.

But God had heard his prayer all along. In fact, God was already hard at work answering Habakkuk's prayer. The king of

Babylon had overturned the Assyrian empire and was going from place to place, subduing one nation after another. Habakkuk and his people's turn to be subdued would be soon. These words were addressed to the Jews, for them to consider and regard the work God was doing, and His providence among the nations of the earth.

The work God was doing among the nations in Habakkuk's day was the destruction of the Jewish nation, city, and temple by the Chaldeans. In some ways, it was a terrifying work, but it was still the work of divine providence being done according to the will of God and by His direction.

Some of the people living then would see it happen and would not believe it could ever have happened, partly because the Chaldeans were their good friends and allies—or so they thought—and partly because they were the covenant people of God, and thought they would never be given up by Him into the hands of another people. So, when they were told of it by the prophets of the Lord, they didn't believe it.

That's what was happening in Habakkuk's day. What is happening in your day or mine may not be as terrifying. Hopefully, the happenings in our lives will be joyful, and the amazing things God is doing that you or I would not have believed if He had told us will be happy and wonderful. The point remains that even when we think God is not hearing our cries to Him, He hears us and is already at work, often in ways we could not imagine.

Isaiah 40:12 says that God measured the earth's waters in the hollow of His hand. How massive and mighty God's hands must be! And, He holds you and me in His hands, too. He loves us, He hears our prayers, and He may already be at work on whatever it is that concerns you and me today.

Prayer: Oh Lord, You are great and mighty! What a blessing to know that You love us and are at work in our lives and in the Word around us, doing great things. Thank You that You hear and answer our prayers. Amen.

Ponder this: Though you may not see it, God is already at work in the situation that concerns you today. Do you find this truth comforting, or are you still frustrated by His lack of an apparent answer? Are you calling out, like Habakkuk, "How long, Lord?" How can you work on waiting patiently?

Day 3
A Simple Prayer
Read: Ezra 8:21-23

There, by the Ahava Canal, I proclaimed a fast, so that we might humble ourselves before our God and ask him for a safe journey for us and our children, with all our possessions.
Ezra 8:21 (NIV)

A new school year was about to begin. In fact, the first day of the new school year was to be the very next day. At the time, I happened to be both a parent and an employee of this Christian school and had been asked to lead in prayer on behalf of the parents at the prayer gathering for the opening of school. I had not prepared for this. The person scheduled to pray came down with some sort of illness, so the organizers of the event called on me at the last minute. I bowed my head and began to pray, and suddenly Ezra's prayer popped into my mind.

Ezra's prayer was a very simple one, but it is perhaps my favorite in the entire Bible. In Ezra 8:22, he confesses that he was ashamed to ask the king for soldiers to protect his group on their journey because he had told the king that God's hand is favorably disposed toward those who fear Him. Ezra had already declared God's faithfulness and promises to the unbelieving king. How would it look after that if he asked the king for help? Surely, it would appear that either Ezra did not really believe what he claimed to believe or that Ezra's God was not so strong after all.

But obviously, Ezra feared what might happen to his group

on their upcoming journey. So, instead of asking for help from men, he asked it from God. Ezra called upon the people to fast and pray. Their prayer was for God's protection over them, their little ones, and their possessions.

What a precious prayer! It covers such earthly things and in so doing, it shows that we can talk to God about everything in our lives—even down to our most basic needs for our health and well-being, our children's health and well-being, and our earthly possessions. How refreshing to realize that God cares about the things that concern us.

As I led in prayer on that warm August evening, standing among the other parents near the flagpole, I recited this Scripture. I reminded God that we, the parents who had gathered to pray the day before the start of this Christian school, were believers. We were His—people who feared Him—as Ezra called it. I said that like Ezra, we were asking for a safe journey through the upcoming school year for our little ones—however big some of those little ones might have become! And, I thanked Him that His gracious hand was upon us and that He answered prayer.

God answered my prayer that year. My little ones are now all safely grown to adulthood. Now, I and they are on new journeys, but I still find myself afraid at times of the dangers we might encounter on these new journeys. It's reassuring to remember this passage and to know that its truths still remain. God still answers prayers and it's still okay to talk to Him about even the most basic things in our lives.

Prayer: Heavenly Father, how thankful we are that Your gracious hand is upon those who fear You! Lord, thank You also for the privilege of bringing any and all of our concerns to You in prayer, in Jesus' name. Amen.

Ponder this: God cares about everything that concerns us. Make a list of your most urgent concerns. Read over it, and remind yourself at each point that God cares about that specific issue.

Day 4
Keeping Your Eyes on God
Read: 2 Chronicles 20:2, 5-6, 12

...For we have no power to face this vast army that is attacking
us. We do not know what to do, but our eyes are on you.
2 Chronicles 20:12 (NIV)

Fear gripped my mother as she walked down the dirt path to the mission hospital in Ogbomoso, Nigeria, where she and my father served as missionaries. I walked behind Mom, next to my little sister, excited to talk to Daddy on the hospital radio, too young to fully understand the danger he was in. I could tell Mom was worried though. Even an eight-year-old could see that. My dad was not with us. He had been sent to relieve the doctors at the hospital in Eku who had been evacuated because of the hospital's proximity to the fighting in the Biafran War that raged nearby.

Every night for two weeks, Mom, my younger sister, Marianne, and I walked the path behind our house to talk with Daddy on the hospital radio. Every night, I heard my sweet daddy's voice and noticed that Mom appeared noticeably frightened on the way there and noticeably relieved on our way home. At the end of his two-week stay, my father came safely back home to us.

What does the Bible say to do when we are gripped by fear? The book of 2 Chronicles tells the story of a time when King Jehoshaphat, one of Judah's kings, faced a situation that had him and his people fearing for their lives. Neighboring armies were marching against Judah fully intending to invade and conquer. What did King Jehoshaphat do?

He prayed!

2 Chronicles 20:3 says he called on the people to fast and then he led them in prayer. I love the way his prayer ends. In verse 12, he says, "We do not know what to do. But our eyes are on You." Maybe he didn't know what to do, but he did the right thing when he turned his eyes and the eyes of the people on God.

Another verse in the Bible makes this clear. 2 Chronicles 14:11 in the New American Standard Bible puts it this way, "Lord, there is no one besides You to help in the battle between the powerful and those who have no strength; so help us, O Lord our God, for we trust in You…"

Does something have you gripped by fear right now? Perhaps things are going well for you right now but a time will surely come when something frightening seems inevitable, turn your eyes to God. As the old hymn, "Turn Your Eyes Upon Jesus" by Helen H. Lemmel, says:

> Turn your eyes upon Jesus,
> Look full in His wonderful face,
> And the things of earth will grow strangely dim,
> In the light of His glory and grace.

During the war in Nigeria when I was a child, my parents and the other missionaries kept their eyes on God. My Dad came home to Ogbomoso safely from Eku, and we made it safely home to America as a family a few years later.

Many times in my adult life, I have been in these shoes, not with physical battles but with spiritual ones. The verse about there being no one besides God to help in battles between the powerful and those who have no strength is one I have committed to memory and quoted back to God in prayers. And God has always proven Himself faithful.

Prayer: Heavenly Father, our eyes are on You. Thank You for being faithful, trustworthy, and a very present help in our times of trouble, in Jesus' name. Amen.

Ponder this: Call on God when you are scared. He is a stronghold in difficult times.

God is God!
Read: 1 Kings 18:24-38

Answer me, Lord, answer me, so these people will know that You,
Lord, are God and that You are
turning their hearts back again.
1 Kings 18:37 (NIV)

Growing up in Africa, I had a keen understanding of false gods even as a young child. Nigeria was filled with many people who worshiped idols. Mine and my family's encounters with idol worship were myriad.

I remember the egunguns that scared me as a child. In its broadest sense, the word simply means "mask" in Yoruba land, where I grew up. But I knew the egungun as a frightening figure. The egungun was actually a man dressed up in masquerade who would dance and leap and whoop around while a group of people gathered around watching and playing drums. He supposedly represented departed spirits but everyone knew he was just a man. They were frightening to me, however. I can remember my father holding me in his arms and walking up to join the circle of people watching an egungun dance. I was really glad when we finally got back in our car!

The ceremony of Oro was different. Oro was not harmless. He represented a more vicious god and during the ceremony which lasted days, people often met their deaths. Most of these were criminals who had been given over to a local group. The condemned were never seen again and their clothes were often found mangled in trees where Oro had supposedly devoured their bodies. Oro's voice was said to sound like a roaring wind and it could be heard the entire length of the ceremony. In actuality, the sound came from a man swinging a rope around and around, making the whirring sound over and over, day and night for days on end. Women were not allowed out during Oro, and because my father had a wife and three daughters, he took no chances. When we heard the whirring coming from the neighboring town, we knew not to leave our mission compound under any circumstances.

With these experiences in my past, it is no wonder a certain story I heard as an adult in Sunday school one day struck me so profoundly. My teacher was discussing the passage in 1 Kings 18 where the prophet, Elijah, called down fire from heaven even when 450 prophets of Baal could not. I had heard this story all of my life but never had I heard it quite like this. My Sunday school teacher, a biblical scholar in his own right, explained something about this passage that I did not know.

He said that in Elijah's day, the people believed in many gods. And these various gods had territories where they were worshiped. The land where the miracle occurred was Baal's territory. It was not Yahweh's territory. He explained that if this very miracle had occurred in Yahweh's territory it would not have seemed quite as amazing to the people. Yahweh could bring about the miracle while Baal remained powerless to do so! It meant that even in Baal's territory, Yahweh ruled!

Then my Sunday school teacher said something that I will never forget. He said, "God is still God, even in Baal's territory!"

We often find ourselves in the territory of other gods, or

more specifically, that old adversary of God, the enemy from the Garden of Eden. Such places exist all over the world. We have places today I would be afraid to travel because of the rampant ungodliness and evil worship of other gods there. We also have places in our lives that the enemy has tried to claim as his.

What does this have to do with prayer? Elijah prayed boldly because he knew that God ruled—always—no matter the location or circumstances. How reassuring to know that God is still God, even in Baal's territory! He is still God even in the enemy's territory. We can pray to Him anywhere, anytime, about anything!

Prayer: Thank You, Lord, that You are the ruler over all things. Thank You for letting us bring all our needs to You, in Jesus' name. Amen.

Ponder this: God rules and overrules! What fears and burdens do you need to lay at His feet today?

Chapter Nine

Other New Testament Prayers

Shirley

Help My Unbelief!
Read: Mark 9:14-28

...I believe, help my unbelief!
Mark 9:24 (NKJV)

When I was in my mid-twenties, a young man whom I had been dating for a while asked me to marry him. It was an exciting evening as we talked about plans for our future. Then, we decided to go show his parents my ring. Since we were each in our own vehicles, and it was thundering and lightning accompanied with hard rain, he suggested I follow him since it would be easier for me to follow the lights of his pick-up truck.

We stopped at a traffic light. His vehicle was the third and mine the fourth. As he slowly made his way into the intersection I saw, seemingly in slow motion, the bright lights coming from the cross street directly toward his vehicle.

The oncoming truck hit his vehicle right at the driver's side door. Both trucks spun wildly out of control. The vehicle carrying my fiancé of twenty minutes wrapped around a telephone pole and stopped.

I put my car in park and ran toward his vehicle. He was not breathing when I reached him. The days, weeks, and months to follow are among the darkest days in my life. I was angry at God, crushed and hurt by my loss.

I tried to read my Bible but ended up staring at the pages without seeing or comprehending any of the words. I just couldn't pray, because I didn't feel like nor believe that God cared about me.

The biblical account we read about in today's passage occurs after an amazing event that Peter, James, and John witnessed— the transfiguration of Jesus when Elijah and Moses appeared.

When Jesus, Peter, James, and John came down to the valley and back to the reality of life, they discovered that the other disciples were unable to cast out a demonic spirit that had made a boy deaf and mute.

In Mark 6:12 we read that Jesus gave the twelve disciples the power to "cast out many demons." So, why couldn't they cast out this demon? It seemed that the disciples' faith was diminishing.

Jesus had always been present with the disciples when they were able to heal someone or cast out demons. This time, Jesus was not with them, because He was up on the mountain. But the time was coming when Jesus would not be with them physically, so their faith needed to be strong in order to continue ministering without Him there. Of course, the Holy Spirit remained, but they had become dependent upon Jesus being there physically.

Jesus told the father to bring the boy to Him. When the demon saw Jesus, he threw the boy into convulsions. Jesus asked the father how long this had been happening. He didn't ask because He didn't know the answer. Jesus asked so that He could show His compassion to the father and the boy.

The father says, "If you can do anything, have compassion on us and help us." The fact that this father brought His son to Jesus shows he did have faith, but his statement showed his faith was weak.

In the next verse, Jesus asks the child's father, and us, do you have the faith to believe that the Lord can do this—or anything else?

The father immediately said, "I do believe! Help my unbelief!" The father understood that his faith was weak.

That is what I was feeling. I believed that God loved me and that He was in control. I was having a difficult time stretching that belief to real trust and faith to believe that while things around me were horrible, He was still walking beside me.

Even Christ-followers who have been long-time followers of Christ have difficulty believing and trusting in God and His Word at times. In praying "help my unbelief," we admit that we can only believe as we should in the strength, grace, and mercy of God.

Prayer: Thank You, Father, for my faith. May it grow, strengthen and be sustained. May it never fail. I pray that my faith in You will be powerful so that You will be glorified in and through everything, in Jesus' name. Amen.

Ponder this: God is the sustainer of our faith, so pray He would sustain your faith and the faith of others. Ephesians 3:14-19 tells us that Father God strengthens our inner man and that through faith Christ dwells in our hearts.

All I Want is You!
Read: Luke 10:38-42

"But one thing is needed, and Mary has chosen that good part,
which will not be taken away from her."
Luke 10:42 (NKJV)

While eating lunch at a local restaurant, I watched and listened to the interaction among those seated a few tables over from me. A little girl who looked about eight years old and her brother who looked about six were sitting with their dad. The children kept asking how long it would be before their grandma got there and they could eat. Their dad kept answering, "She is on her way, she'll be here soon."

The fifth time the children asked when their grandma would be there, in a somber voice their dad answered, "Grandma will be here soon. Now listen, I have to ask her to help us, so please behave well."

The children got busy talking about the pancakes they were going to eat as they pointed to pictures in the menu of what they wanted. Grandma arrived soon, and after all the hugs, she told the children she was buying their breakfast and they could get whatever they wanted.

My lunch arrived, and I got busy eating. Then, something Grandma said caught my ear. It was apparently close to the little boy's birthday because Grandma asked him, "What do you want for your birthday?"

I could tell by the serious look on the little boy's face that he was giving a great deal of thought to how he should answer. Just as the little boy took a deep breath and started to answer, his dad interjected, "Son, you know how tight money is right now, so don't get your hopes too high. Ask for something small, okay?"

Grandma said, "I'm asking what he wants me to get him."

Again, in a gentle but firm voice, the dad said, "Son, ask for something small."

With barely a moment's wait, the little boy jumped down from his chair and ran around the table to his dad, threw his arms around him and said, "All I want is you! I love you, Daddy!"

I began thinking about all the times I run to my Heavenly Father. I go to Him when I am afraid, confused, lonely, angry, sad, and many other times, which is precisely what He invites us to do. Yet, I seldom run to Him in humble recognition that He is all I need.

This interaction between the little boy and his daddy was such a wonderful picture of what God, our Heavenly Father, desires from us—His children.

Today's passage tells us about two sisters, Martha and Mary, who welcomed Jesus into their home. Martha was busy getting the meal prepared so everyone could eat. In contrast, her sister Mary sat at Jesus' feet listening carefully to everything He said and worshiping Him as she anointed His feet with oil.

While Martha was consumed with and distracted by getting the meal prepared and served, Mary was consumed with the person of Jesus Christ. Her focus was on Jesus, so she sat quietly at His feet and listened. And, she worshiped Him as a result of the things she was learning about who He was.

In today's focal passage, Jesus reprimands Martha for being

so distracted with everything in the kitchen that she wasn't listening to Him. He tells Martha that her sister Mary was actually doing the one thing that needed to be done—focusing completely upon Him as she sat at His feet, learned from Him and worshiped Him.

As Mary came to Jesus, not to receive healing or anything else, she was indicating that she understood who He was and that He was all that she needed—in Him she was complete.

Jesus invites us to come "sit at His feet" and learn from Him through His Word and to fellowship and communicate with Him through prayer.

What our Heavenly Father desires is for us to come to Him saying, "All I want is you, Father!"

Prayer: Our Gracious Heavenly Father, thank You for inviting and allowing us to know You. Give us a desire to know You better. Increase our love for You and our desire to spend time communicating with You through prayer, in Jesus' name. Amen.

Ponder this: Jesus, the Savior of the world, invites us to "sit at His feet" to learn from Him through His Holy Spirit-inspired Word, fellowship and communicate with Him through prayer, and to worship Him.

Be Persistent in Prayer

Read: Luke 18:1-8

Continue earnestly in prayer,
being vigilant in it with thanksgiving.
Colossians 4:2 (NKJV)

Because of my connections with several area churches, on any given day I usually know of at least one person who is either in the hospital or who has a loved one in the hospital. Through personal experience, I have learned the importance of having family and friends check on us, so I make a point to check on others when they are in the hospital.

Some time ago, I went to an area hospital to visit a lady who had a massive stroke. When I arrived in her ICU room, her brother, whom I had met numerous times, was there watching over his sister. The neurologist walked in shortly after me. I introduced myself as a friend from church and said I would step out while he was in the room. He said I didn't need to leave, he just wanted to check a couple of things. The doctor began explaining to the brother that there was some very slight improvement, but that she was still in critical condition.

The brother said, "Well, I know God's gonna heal her because he's gonna get tired of hearing her name!"

"What?" responded the doctor, with a puzzled look on his face.

The brother went on to explain, "So many people are praying

for my sister that God will get tired of hearing her name and just heal her!"

The doctor gave a kind nod as he walked out of the room. I stood by this precious lady's bedside, held her hand and prayed aloud for her, after which I left the room also.

Questions kept rolling over in my mind, "Does God really work that way? Does He grow sick and tired of hearing our prayer requests?" Let's see what Scripture teaches us about prayer.

As was His custom, Jesus spoke in a parable in today's passage. This parable comes at the end of a conversation Jesus had with His disciples, as he answered a question the Pharisees asked, and then began telling the disciples what would happen at the second coming of Christ.

Then, Jesus told the disciples to be persistent in their prayers and to not lose heart regardless of how unbearable things appeared. To illustrate this truth, he told this parable about the persistent widow and a judge who, although he was responsible to uphold the law of God and to be respectful and show compassion toward the people who came before him, "did not fear God nor regard man."

The widow kept coming before the judge saying the same thing over and over, "Avenge me of mine adversary."

The judge would not help this widow. He apparently had no interest in upholding God's law and in showing compassion to anyone—even a destitute widow. But finally, because the woman's continual presence and bold requests were wearing him out, he gave in and gave her justice.

Jesus was telling the disciples that between His first and second coming, although things would get rough, they were not to lose hope but to pray. For us today, his meaning is applicable: regardless of all the things happening around us, we are not to lose heart, but to be persistent in prayer. Until Christ comes again, we are to pray for strength to stand against the desires of our flesh, the pulls of the world and the evil one, the hatred of our God and the gospel, and persecution.

There are two important things to remember: prayer is communing with God, and every prayer of a Christ-follower is answered. Sometimes the answer is yes, sometimes it is no, sometimes the answer is not now, other times the answer is something completely different from what we thought was best.

This parable reminds us that if the wicked judge could not ignore the widow's persistent request, we know that our holy and righteous Heavenly Father will certainly listen to His children.

God answered our prayers for the lady who had the massive stroke, not because He got tired of hearing her name, but because of His mercy and grace. She has only minimal long-term effects of the stroke.

God does not grow sick and tired of hearing our prayers! In fact, this passage makes it clear that we are to be persistent in our prayers. The admonition to be persistent in prayer means to live our lives in active recognition that God is a loving Father. He is in control and is always with us, so we can talk to Him any time of the day or night about anything at all! It doesn't matter how trivial something seems to us, God tells us to bring all our cares and concerns to Him in prayer.

Prayer: Father, thank You that You do not get tired of us when we come to You with our requests. Give us wisdom to know the things for which we should pray persistently. In the name of

Jesus, we pray. Amen.

Ponder this: We are told to be persistent in our prayers, but are we persistent in praying for the things that please the Lord? In our persistence are we seeking God's will or our own desires?

Comfort Those in Trouble
Read: I Corinthians 1:3-4

Therefore, we do not lose heart.
Even though our outward man is perishing,
yet the inward man is being renewed day by day.
2 Corinthians 4:16

I had read today's focal passage many times but had never really understood and experienced what it meant until March 1986, when my big brother Paul and his son Little Tim were killed in a train accident.

As you can imagine, it was a horrendous time in my family's life. Hundreds of our family and friends from around the world gathered around us. A dear friend was at Mom and Dad's when I drove in from my home in Nashville that Sunday morning. She barely left my side for the next three days as she watched over me and anticipated my every need.

Numerous other times during critical situations in my life and the life of my family, dear friends have come to us and comforted us. Here are just a few examples.

A dear friend bought my plane ticket home when my dad had his stroke. Another friend met me at the airport in Birmingham when I arrived from Washington, DC, and drove me to Gadsden late that night. Dad died several hours after I arrived at the hospital. Another friend drove from Atlanta to Gadsden for my dad's funeral. During the visitation, funeral, and burial, this friend was always standing where I could see him and know that he was there for me.

For weeks, I was in the hospital getting well enough for surgery to remove a diseased kidney, for the surgery itself, and a little recovery time. Numerous times during that long hospital stay, three special friends came to my room, pulled the chair up by my bed, and held my hand. Sometimes, I slept the whole time they were there. Other times, I was in such pain I just moaned and groaned. During all of this, my friends would read Scripture, pray aloud, and sing hymns.

Friends kept vigil at the burn trauma unit waiting room with us when my nephew was critically burned. They even brought Cracker Barrel chicken and dumplings for supper one night!

My aunt, Mom's baby sister, and uncle came to Birmingham to spend the night with Mom and me and then drove us to the visitation and funeral for my big brother, Tim (for whom Little Tim was named). That night we told stories, and laughed and cried together.

Three precious friends came to the apartment Mom and I shared on the morning Mom died. They cleaned out my refrigerator to make room for the food that would be coming, straightened and cleaned the apartment, and they even rearranged the living room to help better accommodate any guests who would be coming.

Wait! This is supposed to be about prayer, right? What do of all of these examples have to with prayer?

Each of these ministry acts was very intentional. These various Christ-followers were staunch men and women of prayer. Because of the richness of their own prayer life and walk with Christ, they were able to dispense the comforting grace, love, and encouragement we needed in every situation.

The passage we read praises God the Father for His comfort in the midst of our troubles. Furthermore, it tells us that because we experienced something troubling for which we needed comfort from God, we learned how to comfort others when they are troubled.

God used these many friends to encourage me and my family to "not lose heart." How did they do that? First, they were diligent to be in the Word, to pray, and to be quick to confess and repent of their sin so that their relationship with Christ remained unhindered. Each one recognized his or her spiritual gifts, as well as God-given talents and abilities and readily used them when opportunities arose. They joyfully served the Savior as they ministered to and comforted me and my family spiritually, emotionally, mentally, and physically.

These friends prayed fervently and consistently for and with us. So, although we were often "perishing" outwardly, our souls were being renewed by the power and Word of God so that we did not lose heart, but placed our absolute hope in the only real source of hope—Jesus Christ.

Prayer: Father, I thank You for the comfort You bring us when we are troubled. And, I thank You that through Your comfort, we learn how to comfort others who are troubled, in Jesus' name. Amen.

Ponder this: How have your fellow Christ-followers brought comfort to you and your family? Do you take time out of your busy life to bring comfort to those in need?

Standing in the Gap
Read: Colossians 4:12-13

Therefore, confess your sins to each other
and pray for each other so that you may be healed.
The prayer of a righteous person is powerful and effective.
James 5:16 (NIV)

Decades ago, I met a lady with whom I soon became close friends. This precious lady loved the Lord, her family, her church, and she had a passion for missions. The Sunday I joined the church where she was a member, the pastor introduced me as a missionary kid. This woman made a bee-line for me at the close of the service. She wanted to know more about where my parents were missionaries and how long they were on the mission field, what their assignment was, and more.

We forged a close friendship, and I soon learned she was faithful in praying and standing in the gap for not only missionaries but many others throughout the world. She always seemed to know what to pray, when she needed to pray, and for what to pray. She studied missions and prayed for the missionaries and their families and the people to whom they were ministering.

In the passage you read today, Paul tells the Colossians that Epaphras had been wrestling in prayer for them so that they would be able to stand firm in God's will. Epaphras loved his brothers and sisters in Christ. That love impelled him to pray fervently for them.

Today's focal passage tells us that Christ-followers are to be open and honest with each other about our struggles and to pray for each other.

The better we know Christ and the closer our relationship with Him is, the more we will be compelled or drawn to pray for others. That same knowledge and relationship compel or boost our desire to pray for others—to stand in the gap for them.

What does it mean to stand in the gap for someone? It means that we pray and plead on behalf of someone.

There are examples of people who were willing to stand in the gap for their people or family or friends. Sometimes our standing in the gap is praying for God's mercy and forgiveness for others, for God's strength to carry them through a trial, and sometimes we need to stand in the gap as we pray that the darkness of a person's sin would be exposed.

Within the church, it is vital that we stand in the gap for our church leaders and members. We need to be praying about their physical health issues, yes, but that isn't all! We need to pray for their spiritual health, for their strength to withstand attacks of the devil, for their faith to grow, for them to become aware of their sin, and many other things.

A note in the margin of my Bible (I do not know who said it) says, "Intercession can restore and build a spiritual wall of protection." How often do you pray for the spiritual protection of your family and church family as they go out into the world of darkness and sin?

Another note in the margin of my Bible asks, "Is God calling you to stand in the gap?" Underneath I have written, "Well, duh!" Meaning, yes, throughout the Bible God calls us to stand in the gap for others.

Prayer: Heavenly Father, give us a passion to know You better so that our relationship with You is closer. Give us a passion to stand in the gap for others. Give us eyes and ears to see and hear the things with which others are dealing where we need to stand in the gap. In the name of Jesus, I pray. Amen.

Ponder this: We must stand firm in our own faith, and, stand in the gap for others. Who are the people whom God has placed in your life? What are some ways you can stand in the gap for them?

Chapter Ten
Prophet and Wisdom

Harriet

The Splendor of His Majesty
Read: Job 5:8-16

He alone stretches out the heavens and treads on the waves of the sea. He is the Maker of the Bear and Orion, the Pleiades and the constellations of the south. He performs wonders that cannot be fathomed, miracles that cannot be counted.
Job 9:8-10 (NIV)

My father used to tell me about the stars. He knew every constellation by name and would point to each, telling me its name and story. I loved to go walking with him on clear, warm nights.

Back in Nigeria in the 1960s, when we lived there, electricity was scarce and the skies seemed clearer because of the lack of artificial light. I had a little friend whose dad loved to look at the stars, too, and he gladly shared with us something we didn't have—a telescope!

The only constellation that really stuck in my head as a child was Orion—the warrior who died from a scorpion bite. I understood how dangerous scorpion bites could be. Though most scorpion bites do not have enough venom to actually kill a person, they can cause painful, swollen local reactions. And, some bites can, in fact, be lethal, especially to a child. Growing up in Africa, I knew to watch out for scorpions. To this day, I find myself glancing inside my shoes before I put them on my feet, for that elusive scorpion that might be lurking there... but one never is, since I now live in America, in a state too cold for scorpions.

The constellation of Orion was easy to spot with its three stars in a row that made up the great warrior's belt. The memory of my dad pointing to the stars in the bright African skies still gives me pause. The warm tropical night skies came alive with tiny twinkling lights all over it. I used to always think how glorious and mighty God must be to have placed those stars in the sky! Psalm 145:5 described it well when it spoke of the glorious splendor of God's majesty.

This was Job's conclusion, too. In fact, God's glorious majesty was a source of some confusion for Job. He pondered how a lowly man, the created, could ask things of the Creator God, so glorious, so strong, so sovereign. Yet, Job concluded that God was his only hope. In verse 16 of today's passage Job said that because of God's greatness, the helpless have hope. And in Job 13:15 he went one step further when he said, "Though He slay me, I will hope in Him. Nevertheless I will argue my ways before Him" (NASB).

Job's comment makes me chuckle. He basically was saying, "Though he slay me, I will hope in Him… and until He takes my life, I'll keep on praying to Him constantly and begging Him for a favorable answer to my prayers!"

I've been in Job's shoes. I have had times in my life when my situation or that of a loved one for whom I was praying seemed utterly hopeless. But as long as I had breath, I continued to cry out to God about the situation. Like Job, I knew He was my only hope.

What is heavy on your heart and mind today? God wants to hear about it. Job 34:21 says, "His eyes are on the ways of mortals; He sees their every step" (NIV).

I have a friend who likes to say, "God's got this." I think that's what Job was trying to tell us. God's got this. His eyes are on us, He hears our prayers, and He is our only hope.

Prayer: Oh, Glorious Father, Maker of the heavens and the earth, Your splendor knows no bounds. You know what we are going through, and You know our every need. Help us to place our trust in You today. You are our only hope, in Jesus' name. Amen.

Ponder this: God's got this. What are you holding tightly onto and trying to solve by yourself? Or will you consciously turn it over to God today?

Day 2

Job's Restoration
Read: Job 42:10-17

After Job had prayed for his friends, the Lord restored his fortunes and gave him twice as much as he had before.
Job 42:10 (NIV)

The book of Job is very familiar to most Christians. However, there is a special lesson about prayer buried in Job's story that is not so familiar. In fact, this little nugget of wisdom is usually overlooked by those reading or studying the book of Job.

Job experienced tremendous adversity! He lost his children, his personal wealth, and even his health. He lost everything except his wife and his faith. During his trials, Job's friends were anything but helpful! In fact, they drew God's anger with their notoriously bad advice and false statements. Nevertheless, at the end of the book, God did a work of restoration in Job's life.

Job 42:7-12 tells us, "…the Lord said to Eliphaz the Temanite: 'My anger burns against you and your two friends, for you have not spoken of me what is right, as my servant Job has… And my servant Job shall pray for you, for I will accept his prayer not to deal with you according to your folly…' So Eliphaz and Bildad and Zophar went and did what the Lord had told them, and the Lord accepted Job's prayer. And the Lord restored the fortunes of Job when he prayed for his friends. And the Lord gave Job twice as much as he had before."

Eliphaz, Bildad, and Zophar were three of Job's closest

friends; but unfortunately, they offered him very poor advice throughout his personal ordeal. At the end of the book, God held them accountable while at the same time exonerating Job. This is how most people remember the story's end. The friends face the truth of their shortcomings, Job is honored, and God restores back to Job twice as much as he had before. This understanding of the end of Job's story is accurate, but there is something more.

Today's key verse, Job 42:10 (NIV), says, "After Job had prayed for his friends, the Lord restored his fortunes and gave him twice as much as he had before." The restoration of Job's fortunes occurred *after* he prayed for his friends. That certainly drives home the importance of praying for others!

My prayer group jokingly calls this the "Job method" of praying. We tease that our prayers for others are selfishly motivated because we are hoping that, like Job, God will restore our fortunes too, as we pray for our friends. Actually, there is no simple formula to prayer. The study and practice of prayer are multifaceted—but the importance of praying for others is one facet we would do well to remember.

It's natural to focus on our needs or problems when we pray. After all, that is what we see most clearly and feel most deeply. Praying for others may be a habit we need to work at learning. This little lesson from Job surely gives me motivation. It illustrates the fact that God blesses us when we see the needs of others, pray, and minister to them.

Prayer: Lord, open our eyes to the needs around us. Show us specific ways we can pray for and help others. Thank You that You bless us when we lift up others, in Jesus' name. Amen.

Ponder this: Who do you know that needs your prayers today? Do you know their specific needs? If not, find out. Have you told someone you would pray for them? Have you really prayed like you said you would?

A Stronghold in Times of Trouble
Read: Nahum 1:3-7

*The Lord is good, a stronghold in the day of trouble, and He
knows those who take refuge in Him.*
Nahum 1:7 (NASB)

The Nigerian-Biafran War I experienced as a child is vivid in
my memory and shows up often in my various writing endeavors.
Because I was so young, I sometimes was not fully aware of the
dangers around me at the time they were happening. They often
felt more like inconveniences, than dangers. Looking back,
however, I realize just how precarious things were at times. My
parents, of course, were keenly aware of the dangers. They had
answered God's call to foreign missions, never suspecting that it
would land them in a war zone.

I could sometimes see how the war affected the country as
well as our mission efforts. I was aware that my parents seemed
to be in a constant state of heightened concern and, whenever we
traveled, we started encountering roadblocks with armed soldiers,
something that had never happened before.

On one such roadblock/armed soldier encounter that I
remember vividly, the soldier looked in the back seat of our car
and saw me sitting there. He opened the door, picked me up in
his arms, and rested me on his hip. I was all of about eight years
old. He stroked my blonde hair and told my dad that he wanted to
take me to be his bride.

My father knew the customs and language of the Yoruba people with whom we lived. He told the soldier, in Yoruba, in a joking manner, that my bride-price was far too high. The soldier threw back his head and laughed heartily. Then he told my dad to name my price. Daddy quickly informed the man that he could never afford me—my bride-price was so high even kings could not afford me. The man laughed again and placed me back on the car, telling my parents they could move on.

I remember being in that man's arms. But I wasn't frightened because my dad was standing only a few feet from me. I fully believed that he wouldn't let any harm come to me. From my father's point of view, it must have felt quite different, yet he kept his cool. He managed to laugh and joke with the man in a language and about customs the man understood. In the end, my earthly father and my Heavenly Father protected me.

Why were my parents able to confidently remain in that war-torn country? It was because they and the other missionaries who served alongside them took refuge in their Lord. They knew, as our key verse says, God knows those who take refuge in Him. And like the prophet Nahum, my parents also knew that their God was a stronghold in times of trouble.

What war zone are you in today? Is yours a relationship war, a financial war, or maybe a spiritual war of some other type? Maybe you feel attacked on all sides. Does an enemy have you in his arms trying to claim you as his? Rest assured, God sees what you are going through. Jeremiah 12:3 says this in plain words. And Jeremiah 33:3 tells us that we can call upon God and He will answer. Prayer is your weapon.

Prayer: Heavenly Father, thank You for the truths in Your Word.

Thank You for being a stronghold for those who take refuge in You. Teach us to turn to You in our days of trouble. Amen.

Ponder this: God knows those who take refuge in Him. He sees what we are going through and He answers when we call to Him. What do you need to turn over to God today?

The Day of Small Things
Read: Zechariah 4:6-10

The prophet Zechariah asks the question,
"For who has despised the day of small things?"
Zechariah 4:10 (NASB)

"Mom! I'm bored!" This exclamation came from my then twelve-year-old son just two weeks after school ended for summer break. My, how quickly a child can become bored. Frankly, becoming bored with the mundane is something adults experience, too.

The prophet Zechariah poses the question, "Who has despised the day of small things?" One answer to this question would be my twelve-year-old son. But the question is a good one to be pondered by all. What are the days of small things? These are days when nothing much seems to have happened in our lives. We are a people who yearn for excitement, especially in today's fast-paced world. We would do well to learn to appreciate days when nothing of significance occurs—days of small things.

In the Scripture's context, the day of small things actually meant a day when it seemed the people had accomplished nothing. They were working on rebuilding the temple—what would become known as Zerubbabel's temple. Back in those days, all construction was done with basic manual labor; brick by brick, literally. The people worked day-in and day-out but the walls went up so slowly that at the end of many of the days, they felt as if they were not accomplishing anything.

God tells them through Zechariah, the prophet, not to grumble about the days of small things. They were accomplishing more than they realized. The work they were doing was valuable work, even if it seemed painfully slow. In verse 6 of chapter 4, God told the people the work was happening by much more than their labor when He said (NIV), "This is the word of the Lord to Zerubbabel: 'Not by might nor by power, but by my Spirit,' says the LORD Almighty."

Prayer can be like that sometimes. We pray about something day after day, and it feels like we do not see any answers. I find this verse quite comforting. It motivates me to keep praying. I picture myself laying down one row of bricks on that temple. It's a grand work that God is doing, and my prayers are a part of it!

In fact, some of my specific prayers have been for loved ones who struggled in some area. The days that nothing happens—those really boring days—have become treasured days to me. They are answered prayers, because, for that day, God prevented the struggle from overwhelming my loved one.

I've grown to love ordinary days—mornings when we wake up to nothing unusual. Days I face the ordinary challenges of home, work, and church life. I go to work, come home, eat dinner with my family, help the children or grandchildren with homework, attend Bible study or choir practice… just my usual weekly activities. What a blessing these days are! Then we crawl into our warm, safe bed for a good night's sleep in the home God has provided, ever mindful that I was not called to the home of someone in dire need or to a hospital bed of a loved one. I am ever thankful for the extraordinary God who has allowed me to live another ordinary day.

Prayer: Father, we thank You for all of the normal and ordinary days in our lives. Teach us to live each of them for You, in Jesus' name. Amen.

Ponder this: God gives us ordinary days and not-so-ordinary ones. Some days we feel our prayers aren't being answered while other days we see miraculous answers. May we learn to wait on the Lord and treasure those days of small things that He gives us.

He has made everything beautiful in its time. He has also set eternity in the human heart; yet no one can fathom what God has done from beginning to end. Ecclesiastes 3:11 (NIV)

"Special."

That word was written in large letters on a sign taped to the side of a bus that sat in a used vehicle lot in Tegucigalpa, Honduras. The mission team purchased the bus for the church in La Paz, Honduras, with whom they had worked many summers. The students on the high school mission trip that year decided Special was a good name for the bus. The name stuck, and for many years afterward, other mission teams, too, as well as the church members, fondly called this bus Special.

One summer, a few years ago, I had the privilege of participating in this annual student trip as a chaperone. It's a trip by the students of the Christian school where I have been a parent for many years and also work as a substitute teacher. I'm a registered nurse, though I am not currently employed in that capacity. But I do have a bachelor's degree in nursing, and that year they needed a nurse to come along, so they asked me. What a blessing that trip turned out to be!

Having now spent time in Special, I can assure you she is well named! She has a cracked windshield that cannot be replaced because a piece of glass with the correct dimensions is difficult, if not impossible, to find in Honduras. Her ability to keep running is occasionally affected by one thing or another. Sometimes, Special develops problems which require attention. On our way to the airport to catch our flight home, Special stopped running altogether, and the church had to quickly find us alternate transportation.

Nevertheless, most of the time Special faithfully goes up and down winding, dirt, and mountainous roads every week to bring people to church who would otherwise not be able to worship. I remember seeing the bus driver turn Special around on the narrowest of roads on a sharp hill after picking up children for a church activity. I didn't know how Special made it, but she always did.

Zechariah 14:20-21 speaks of the holiness of even the cups and cooking pots in the temple. Indeed, God's purpose for all things is their holiness. I suppose if cups and cooking pots can be special to the Lord, then so can an old bus with a cracked windshield.

God's people are a bit like that, too. God's purpose for us is holiness, and we are all special in our own ways. God created us differently for His unique purposes, and he loves our specialness.

Have you discovered what God's special purpose for you is? Maybe it's to be a prayer warrior. Though all Christians are called to pray, I truly believe that for some, the ability to know prayer needs and to lift them up regularly is a special purpose God calls them to. My parents are some of these people. Their prayers are consistent and powerful. As they age, they are less able to do some of the other things they have done in their lives, but they still pray with vigor and conviction. Perhaps that's why God has blessed them with such long lives.

Prayer: Heavenly Father, thank You for the uniqueness of Your plan for each of our lives. Help us to appreciate our own specialness and that of others, in Jesus' name. Amen.

Ponder this: God makes everything beautiful in its time. His purpose for all things is their holiness, and He has called each to a special work for Him. What is God calling you today?

Now What?

You have completed the fifty meditations about prayer from the Old Testament and New Testament. Now, what do you do?

First of all, PRAY! You've read about and meditated upon prayer through these devotions, so don't forget to actually pray.

We recommend that you continue being transformed by the continual renewing of your mind through the Holy Spirit-inspired Word of God (Romans 12:1-2) by being diligent and consistent in your personal reading, studying, memorizing, contemplating, and meditating upon His Word. Find a plan (many are available online) for a systematic reading so that you read through the entire Bible.

If you would like a deeper study of prayer, we recommend, *Prayer: It's Not About You* by Harriet E. Michael and the *Study Guide on Prayer—A Companion to Prayer: It's Not About You* by Shirley Crowder.

For the busy holiday season we recommend, *Glimpses of the Savior: 30 Meditations on Thanksgiving, Christmas, and the New Year* by Shirley Crowder and Harriet E. Michael.

Choose another devotional to begin, use a book and/or study guide on a specific biblical topic, or choose a book of the Bible and begin reading and studying it on your own with help from the internet.

On the following page, you will find recommended resources: devotionals, books, and study guides/workbooks that will help you continue your study of the Bible.

The real issue is not how we are praying
but whether.

Begin!
How the devil loves to hear us
talk about tomorrow.

Alistair Beggs

Recommended Reading

Books about Prayer

A Call to Prayer – J. C. Ryle

A Call to Spiritual Reformation: Priorities from Paul and His Prayer – D. A. Carson

A Woman's Call to Prayer: Making Your Desire to Pray a Reality – Elizabeth George

Disciplines of a Godly Man – R. Kent Hughes

Hudson Taylor's Spiritual Secret – Dr. Hudson Taylor

Life and Diary of David Brainerd – Edited: Jonathan Edwards

Pray About Everything: Cultivating God-Dependency –Paul Tautges

Prayer: Experiencing Awe and Intimacy with God – Tim Keller

Prayer: It's Not About You – Harriet E. Michael

Study Guide on Prayer—A Companion to Prayer: It's Not About You – Shirley Crowder

Praying Backwards – Bryan Chapell

Praying the Bible – Donald S. Whitney

Praying the Names of God – Ann Spangler

Reaching the Ear of God: Praying More and More Like Jesus – Wayne A. Mack

Spurgeon on Prayer – Charles Spurgeon

The Autobiography of George Muller – George Muller

The Complete Works of E. M. Bounds on Prayer – E. M. Bounds

The Heart of Prayer – Jerram Barrs

The Mighty Weakness of John Knox – Douglas Bond

With Christ in the School of Prayer – Andrew Murray

With the Master: On Our Knees – Susan J. Heck

Devotionals

A Shelter in the Time of Storm: Meditations on God and Trouble – Paul David Tripp

Cross Talking: A Daily Gospel for Transforming Addicts – Mark E. Shaw

Face to Face: Praying the Scriptures for Intimate Worship – Kenneth D. Boa

Face to Face: Praying the Scriptures for Spiritual Growth – Kenneth D. Boa

Glimpses of the Savior – Shirley Crowder & Harriet E. Michael

Hearing and Answering God: Praying Psalms 1-75 – Stephen D. Cloud

My Utmost for His Highest – Oswald Chambers

New Morning Mercies: A Daily Gospel Devotional – Paul David Tripp

The Quiet Place: Daily Devotional Readings – Nancy DeMoss Wolgemuth

Through Baca's Valley – J. C. Philpot

Valley of Vision: A Collection of Puritan Prayers – Arthur G. Bennett

Whiter Than Snow: Meditations on Sin and Mercy – Paul David Tripp

About the Authors

Shirley Crowder

Shirley Crowder was born in a mission guest house under the shade of a mango tree in Nigeria, West Africa, where her parents served as missionaries. She and co-author Harriet E. Michael grew up together on the mission field and have been lifelong friends. Shirley is passionate about disciple-making, which is conducted in and through a myriad of ministry opportunities.

She is a biblical counselor and co-host of "Think on These Things," a Birmingham, Alabama, radio/TV program for women. Shirley is commissioned by and serves on the national advisory team for The Addiction Connection. Several of her articles have appeared in "Paper Pulpit," in the Faith section of "The Gadsden Times," and in a David C. Cook publication. She has authored and co-authored several books.

Shirley has spiritual children, grandchildren, and great-grandchildren serving the Lord in various ministry and secular positions throughout the world.

Follow her on:
Facebook: **www.facebook.com/shirleycrowder**
Twitter: **www.twitter.com/ShirleyJCrowder**
Blog: **www.throughthelensofScripture.com**
Amazon: **www.amazon.com/author/shirleycrowder**

Harriet E. Michael

Harriet E. Michael was born in Joinkrama, Nigeria, deep in the African jungle in the Niger River Delta, where her father served as the only missionary doctor at that station. A few years later, the mission moved the family to a larger hospital in Ogbomoso. Co-author, Shirley Crowder, and her family lived right across the dirt road. The two children became constant playmates. Today, they continue to enjoy their lifelong friendship.

Harriet is a prolific nonfiction writer, having penned close to 200 articles, devotions, and stories. Her work has appeared in publications by Focus on the Family, David C. Cook, Lifeway, Standard Publishing, Chicken Soup for the Soul, The Upper Room, Judson Press, and more. She has also authored or co-authored several books.

She and her husband of over 38 years have four children and two grandchildren. When not writing, she enjoys substituting at a Christian school near her home, gardening, cooking, and traveling.

Follow her on:

Facebook: **www.facebook.com/harrietmichaelauthor**
Blog: **www.harrietemichael.blogspot.com**
Amazon: **amazon.com/author/harrietemichael**

About the Illustrator

Kristin Michael

Kristin is a freelance artist whose preferred medium is oil painting. Her style is contemporary expressionist with a focus on light and water. She obtained her liberal arts degree at Bellarmine University in Louisville, Ky with a double minor in fine arts and literature.

Kristin continued her education at St. Catherine College in Bardstown, KY where she earned an associate degree in Cardiac Sonography.

She is now employed full-time by Ky Children's Hospital as a pediatric and adult congenital cardiac sonographer (she performs ultrasounds on children and adults with congenital heart disease).

Kristin works hard in her healthcare and artistic endeavors as a single mother in order to take care of her sweet young son who is the light of her life. You can find more of Kristin's artwork at **www.instagram.com/kiki_paintings**.

Other Pix-N-Pens Devotionals

Dancing Like Bees

31 Steps to De-stress, Delight, and Dance Like Bees

Through the thirty-one devotions, this book examines what Peggy learned about God's intricate creation of the honeybee and how it speaks direction into our need for living peaceful, productive lives while overcoming stress and achieving joy. God is faithful always, and His creation magnifies His majesty if we take time to seek Him in everyday situations—even through the honeybee.

Also by the Authors

Prayer: It's Not About You
by: Harriet E. Michael

Is prayer a mighty spiritual weapon or a waste of time? Is it something to be engaged in fiercely, as if wielding a weapon in the midst of a spiritual battle? Or, is it just a personal practice to achieve a calmer, more focused and disciplined life? Does prayer really change anything?

Those questions and so many more are discussed inside the pages of this book. This study does not simply offer one writer's perspective on the topic of prayer. Instead, it delves deep into Scripture to see how prayer is presented in God's Word.

The book offers a thorough study of prayer from a biblical perspective. Moving from Genesis to Revelation, this book looks at instances of prayer as recorded in the Bible, exploring the who, what, where, when, how, and why.

Available on Kindle and in paperback from Amazon and most bookstores by request.

Study Guide on Prayer

A Companion to Prayer: It's Not About You

by: Shirley Crowder

This study guide is designed to help you study Prayer: It's Not About You, individually or in a group setting. As you work your way through this study guide, you will read the book chapter by chapter. Then you will be guided to interact with the teachings, principles, and practices contained in Scripture and Prayer: It's Not About You.

It is the author's prayer that as you work through this study guide you will gain knowledge and a better understanding of prayer. The Holy Spirit will lead you to incorporate these teachings, principles, and practices into your prayer life so that your passion to pray increases. The result will be a strengthened relationship with God the Father, through Jesus Christ His Son.

Available on Kindle and in paperback from Amazon and most bookstores by request.

Glimpses of the Savior

30 Meditations for Thanksgiving,
Christmas, and the New Year
Finding Jesus Among the Celebrations and Decorations
by: Shirley Crowder and Harriet E. Michael

In early November, we get busy preparing for Thanksgiving, Christmas, and the New Year, and we often forget the real meanings behind these celebrations.

We can guard against this by preparing our hearts to seek Him as we focus on God's Word and by remembering that Thanksgiving is a time to give God thanks; Christmas is the celebration of the Savior's birth; the New Year brings new beginnings. Then, as we go about doing the things the Lord has called us to do where He has called us to do them, we catch Glimpses of the Savior and biblical truth in the things we experience and observe.

These devotionals are based on memories of Thanksgiving, Christmas, and New Year Celebrations in Africa and America. May the Holy Spirit work through these meditations to help readers recognize Glimpses of the Savior in the things they observe, and become skilled at finding Jesus among the celebrations and decorations.

Available on Kindle and in paperback from Amazon and most bookstores by request.

The Whisper of the Palms

by Harriet Michael

Growing up in the foothills of North Carolina, Ali Blackwell dreamed of going places she had only seen in books and magazines. She lived in a small farmhouse that her farmer father had built with his own hands, and the prospects of ever leaving her little town of Union Mills appeared unlikely. Her family barely scraped by on the sale of produce grown by her dad and brothers and the supplemental income they earned working at the nearby textile mill.

Kyle Edmonds, a few years her elder, lived in a larger house in South Carolina. He possessed things Ali only dreamed of—extra clothes and shoes, a house with indoor plumbing and electricity, a family car, a bicycle and other toys, just to name a few.

They could not have been more different.

However, both heard God's still small voice calling them to foreign missions. How will their paths cross? What obstacles will they face? What will their future hold?

Available on Kindle and in paperback from Amazon and most bookstores by request.

Scripture References

Old Testament

New Testament

**Thank you
for reading our books!**

**Look for other books
published by**

Pix-N-Pens Publishing
An imprint of Write Integrity Press
www.WriteIntegrity.com